HIDDEN IMMIGRANTS:

LEGACIES OF GROWING UP ABROAD

BY

LINDA BELL

THE WEST AND THE WIDER WORLD SERIES, VOLUME XI

Cross Cultural Publications, Inc.

CrossRoads Books

Cover Design by Amy Bell

"In Spite of Loss" by Diana Der-Hovanessian
used by permission of the author

The West and the Wider World Series, Volume XI

The West and the Wider World Series features works that describe
the historical processes of inter-cultural relations using Europe as a
point of reference and those that deal with the influence exerted on
Western Civilization by other major civilizations. Editorial Board:
Deno John Geanakoplos, Yale University--Europe, Byzantium and
the Muslim World; Donald F. Lach, University of Chicago--Europe,
Far East and Southeast Asia; Cyriac K. Pullapilly, Saint Mary's
College, Notre Dame (General Editor)--Europe and South Asia

Published by **CROSS CULTURAL PUBLICATIONS, INC.**
Cross Roads Books
Post Office Box 506
Notre Dame, Indiana, 46556, U.S.A.
Phone: (219) 273-6526, 1-800-561-6526
FAX: (219) 273-5973

To Amy and Peggy with Loving Thanks

May Their Journeys Continue

COMMENTS ABOUT "HIDDEN IMMIGRANTS"

Linda Bell's title, **Hidden Immigrants**, *calls attention to a common character-*
istic of adults who have grown up overseas as dependents of American parents
employed abroad. Most have bland exteriors which camouflage rich, complex
and emotion-laden experiences from their childhood and early teen years in
multiple foreign countries.

The exciting insights which emerge from this book concern not what happened
to them, but what each made happen within the constrictions of their time and
place to construct a new identity, a new self and a new occupation out of their
unique set of disjunctive and often painful overseas and American experiences.

> **Professor Emeritus Ruth Hill Useem, PhD**
> **Department of Sociology and Education**
> **Michigan State Univesity**

· · · · ·

This highly readable book will prove useful both to a wide range of behavioral
science professionals and to families seeking information about cultural
adjustment. Linda Bell's compellingly written book provides valuable insights
into the cultural context of development and will undoubtedly spark research
on this understudied area.

> **Professor Janet J. Fritz, PhD**
> **Department of Human Development and Family Studies**
> **Colorado State University**

· · · · ·

The authenticity of these "voices" and Linda Bell, through the pinpoint
accuracy of her insightful commentary, give parents and practitioners an
invaluable resource for undestanding the lifelong impact of a childhood
abroad. Global nomads of all ages will find, as I did, clear affirmation of the
benefits, challenges and value of their internationally mobile heritage.

> **Norma M. McCaig**
> **Founder, Global Nomads International**

· · · · ·

This is certainly a book that all parents living overseas should read. I also think
children should read this book. It would help them to know what other kids in
similar circumstances went through and how they dealt with it. To hear from
a missionary's son and the daughter of a businessman helped me understand
the universality of the children's situations overseas.

> **Fritz Galt, Co-editor of the SUN**
> **(Spouses Underground Newsletter)**

TABLE OF CONTENTS

ACKNOWLEDGEMENTS

First of all, besides the example of my own daughters, I owe the existence of this book to the 13 voices who agreed to talk with me about their experiences growing up. Their candid memories are the backbone of this volume.

Many others made this happen along the way. My thanks and gratitude to Norma McCaig, founder of Global Nomads International, as well as to board members of that organization; to Jewell Fenzi, director of the Foreign Service Spouses Oral History project and author of *Married to the Foreign Service*, who trained me to do oral history; to Mary Edwards Wertsch, author of *Military Brats*, for helping me organize my work and giving me a vocabulary for the task; to Kay Branaman Eakin, former education advisor with the Family Liaison Office at the U.S. Department of State, for championing this project and pushing for its completion; to Jean Larson of Minneapolis for her encouragement and talking me through so many issues, to Elfrieda and Mel Loewen who just happened along at the right time in my life to listen empathetically, and to the many people who read this manuscript in draft and gave me invaluable advice -- Mary Ann Telatnik, Janet Fritz and Lynne Warner of Colorado State University, Fritz Galt of the SUN (Spouses Underground Newsletter), Ruth Obee, Kay Branaman Eakin, my sister Sally Davis, and my daughters Amy and Peggy.

My love and thanks to my husband, Chuck, who has always supported me when I did what I needed to do; and a special thanks to Ed Backus, who offered me a sanctuary in which to work.

In Spite of Loss

The year spins its clay again
toward the potter's hand,
in spite of being conquered
and losing face and stance.

The months crack wide open
 in the cold of the past
but they are smoothed, reshaped,
reglazed, and recast.

The days approach in silence hung
with new leaves, fresh moss.
The year turns to spring again
 in spite of fall and loss.

But there's no trace of you here,
no echo of your steps,
no place, once you have erased
your old return address.

Ardem Haroutiunian
translated from Armenian
by Diana Der-Hovanessian
© Diana Der-Hovanessian

PREFACE

Children who grow up in many different nations -- the children of government officials, businessmen, journalists, missionaries, and others who take their work outside their own countries -- are often the overlooked appendages of adult career choices. While information on the actual childhood experience is increasing, not much is known about how, or if, that experience affects a person lifelong. Or if there are patterns that emerge in the ways people work through it. Is the cultural smorgasbord assimilated or forgotten over time, and if so, how? Does time diminish or heighten the memories and skills? And what does such a person do about roots, if indeed, such a person even needs roots?

Background

Before World War II the number of Americans with overseas careers was smaller than today, and they were generally from a more elite social class. Often these children had strong cultural identities because they were expected to attend American boarding schools from an early age.

Following the war the Marshall Plan opened up the way for more American investment, the American military dug deeply into Europe and Asia for the duration of the Cold War, international forums and organizations burgeoned, and the end of colonialism created a plethora of independent nations which didn't exist before the war. In addition the war resulted in a sudden increase in cross-cultural marriages on both sides of the Atlantic and the Pacific. As a result the number of middle-class Americans working and living overseas increased tremendously during the 1950s and 60s, and continues to grow today. Dr. Ruth Useem of Michigan State University calls the children of these internationally mobile Americans "third culture kids" (TCKs) -- children from one culture, living in other cultures, who among themselves form a third culture which is unique to their experience, has certain ties to their parents' work overseas and is unplaced geographically.

Business and military communities soon recognized the need for overseas American or international schools in the main centers of Europe and Asia. American missionaries already had created such schools in more remote areas. The Department of State picked up the slack through its Office of Overseas Schools, created in 1964. These efforts all reduced the need for children to return to boarding schools in the United States. While our government now does a commendable job briefing employees and families both before going abroad and on return, the business community is less organized as a whole. Some families get excellent preparation, while others get none at all.

Exploring the Legacies

The voices heard in this book are the result of candid, frank conversations with actual individuals. These interviews were taped and transcribed, forming a kind of oral history, rich in emotion, memories and the rhythm of loss and recreation. While not a scientific survey in any way, this is a window into the experience by the people who know it, and can tell it, best. The same stories and themes can be heard in every country of the world by those who return from a childhood outside.

Those who have lived an internationally mobile childhood will be anxious to read about themselves. Younger ones will get a glimpse at what might lay ahead. Those responsible for these children overseas, whether parents, educators, or personnel officers, will gain insights which should help in making decisions affecting the lives of these children.

Often referred to as "hidden immigrants" these individuals are overlooked when it comes to their diversity or marginality because they look and act so American. Yet in mid-life most of them still feel outside the mainstream of American culture. Health professionals, counselors, family development researchers, educators and trainers will in the course of their work probably hear from some of these hidden immigrants. These conversations give them a context with which to listen.

INTRODUCTION

The first time I realized I was in over my head was when my four-year old daughter, Amy, came up to me shortly before we were to depart French West Africa for "home leave" in the States.

"Mommy, what language do they speak in Ohio?" she asked. "Will they understand me?"

Right then I knew that "understand" might be the operable word. Although I assured my daughter that most everyone spoke English in the United States and she would have no trouble communicating, I realized that by her very question she was already very different. Clearly, what we meant, and what she meant, by "home" were quite opposite. After all, she was home, as far as she knew. Amy would, from that very first home leave, be a hidden immigrant, a cultural misfit, in her own country of origin. Already she was set apart by her experiences in ways I couldn't begin to comprehend. I could only try to understand.

By the time Amy was four, she had lived in three countries of North and West Africa. She went to a French school with local and expatriate children, but spoke English at home. She had both English-speaking and French-speaking playmates, but not usually at the same time. She knew she had to speak French to the night guard and gardener, but English to the house staff. Outside her home, communication was in French, not English. At four, her avowed goal was to become an English teacher -- maybe to make her life less complicated! Her affinity group was totally linguistic; race, culture, religion, status or nationality didn't enter into it.

When I told Amy that everybody in America would likely speak English, she was visibly relieved and reassured. But all during that home leave, just to test this, she would walk up to entire strangers and introduce herself; "Hi, I'm Amy Bell and I'm four." Luckily, no one failed to understand or respond in English, but I'm sure no one really understood why she was so intent on greeting them in this way, either.

If our children weren't to have roots, at least they would have a world view. As a mother, I hoped our children could learn to accept cultural diversity with strength and use their knowledge to make the world smaller, more comprehensible. I knew they would be different, but I also assumed those differences would give them something solid in return.

By contrast, my husband and I grew up in the same small town along Lake Erie where we had "landed" roots. We eventually left only when it came time to go to college. It was a lark, an adventure, to be a part of the U.S. Foreign Service when my husband became a commissioned officer in the United States Information Agency.

Both our daughters were born overseas: Amy in Morocco and Peggy in the Ivory Coast almost four years later. Except for home leaves of four to six weeks duration, they never lived in the United States until they were ten and six. By that time their cultural identities had been formed by what we could give them and their years in Africa and Norway.

When they arrived in the United States they could cross-country ski but not play softball, sing the Norwegian national anthem but not the American, explain about kings but not about presidents. When school classmates asked where they'd moved from and they said Norway, the standard response was "Yeah, sure...." When Amy said she couldn't find any friends among her American classmates, we were both skeptical and dismayed. Fortunately, a number of her friends from within the American community in Norway returned to the Washington area about the same time and those friendships helped her make an unenthusiastic transition. She often asked, "When are we going to move overseas again?"

So by default and a little training I became an observer, an amateur social scientist. What would happen to these unlanded children? While we were in the United States from 1977 to 1980, I helped organize a conference -- one of the first of its kind in America and sponsored by the Association of American Foreign Service

Women for the 1979 International Year of the Child -- which focused on the specific needs and problems of internationally mobile children. We wondered, what, if anything, could be done to illuminate the black holes these children could easily fall into as they went on their way? At this conference we found there was even a sociological name for these children. Dr. Ruth Hill Useem of Michigan State University described them as "third culture kids" (TCKs) in her writings in the 1960s.

When the conference ended, and I was preparing to move overseas again, I thought how valuable it would be to have some insights from adults who had gone through this experience as children. I wanted to hear what they had to say from the vantage point of maturity. Were there significant legacies worth noting and exploring, or was cultural mobility just one of those things a person can accept, live through and then move away from? Was there any common ground in the ways these hidden immigrants came to make sense or use of the many cultural and sometimes confusing lessons they had learned as children? Most importantly, what had the experience meant to them?

It wasn't until I returned to the United States in 1990, ten years and three more overseas postings later, that I had the chance to start conducting oral interviews to this end. I started talking to some of the adults I first knew as children in our early overseas postings. From them I got the names of others. I received many other leads networking within the foreign service community. Sometimes I accidentally or serendipitously met someone who had grown up overseas and I would ask to interview them. A few of my interviewees selected themselves through a notice I put in the Global Nomads International Newsletter. My criteria were simple. I asked that my informants were either overseas, or their parents were overseas, during most of their high school years; this holds true for all but one. And I wanted lots of mobility.

My 13 interviewees range in age from 29 to 42, 7 are female and 6 are male. All but two are currently married. Of two who were divorced, one has remarried and the other has not. Two had parents who were themselves raised overseas. None of them had divorced parents, although several have lost a parent due to death. Most of them have had early exposure to other languages, but only one is truly bilingual now. Three of the interviewees come from families of mixed religious origins and minority status. Most have come from the official American foreign affairs community, but one is the child of a missionary, one the child of a businessman, and one the child of a technical specialist overseas on contract. They have lived in from two to eight countries during their childhoods and all of them returned overseas during their late teens and 20s for their own reasons; three as Peace Corps Volunteers, one as a foreign service officer, one as the spouse of a foreign service officer, four on business, several for further education, others to travel. All of them have current passports.

Eight of them were exposed to civil unrest, violence and hardship during their childhoods overseas. Two were sexually intimidated or molested by foreign household servants, three were in boarding schools before they were thirteen. Yet, all but two rate their childhoods as a very positive influence in their lives.

I do not pretend that this is a scientific survey; I am a journalist, not a social scientist. My intent in capturing these oral histories was to open a book and see what transpired on its pages. The perceptions, the insights, the stories come from those who can best describe them. I was not really expecting to find generalities or common solutions. I was not out to prove that this particular way of growing up was good or bad. I just wanted insight into how it was different.

Gradually over the course of the interviews I did start to see some patterns emerge. These patterns, while taking many variations, do seem to fit most of the people I interviewed as they struggled to identify themselves as American and set down roots in this country. These are the ones who have truly entered their own culture. There are many others of course who only return to their home countries long enough to get credentials that enable them to return overseas again, either to countries where they already have language capability and expertise, or just overseas. In those cases, the identity and comfort level as "foreigner" wins out over the identity and perhaps discomfort of being "just" American.

In my interviews I tried to explore mobility and identification issues, the transitions from being a special minority to being mainstream, the effects of mixed cultural signals, the effects of loss and anger and whether those feelings were buried or worked through somehow. I looked at career patterns and the longevity of important relationships. Who were these hidden immigrants marrying, what kinds of people made them feel comfortable and safe? I wanted to know too if they were raising their children differently because of their own childhood experiences. I wanted to know how invested they were in their American lives, if they felt settled or restless after their childhood mobility. I wanted to know about their educations and their careers and if their childhood cultural mobility set them on paths they could identify. I wanted to know if they felt comfortable making new friends. Most of all, I wanted to know if they had regrets or whether they would do it all over again given free choice.

Conditioned to trying to fit in more than to calling attention to themselves, as adults most of these children will be content to go about their lives quietly. After a rocky period, generally in their 20s, these cultural immigrants slowly begin to reconcile their past with their present, their old identities with their newly acquired ones.

Their strength will be in their keen observation and adaptability. They will take risks but resist false authority. They will have sincere empathy for others and the ability to walk in another's shoes.   They will be independent thinkers yet accepting of differences. They will be incredibly loyal to their friends. They will define their roots in terms of people and not be limited to any geographical location.

Their greatest weakness may be an unwillingness to seek help or confide in anyone they haven't known for a very long time. They may have a life-long sense of being out of phase with aspects of their own culture. They may continue to live on the surface, with little community or group involvement outside their work or families. In general, they prefer to be loners rather than gregarious "groupies," and they are sometimes wary of their own power to manipulate others.

Now, as more and more American families go overseas, the need to know the ramifications of cultural mobility seems obvious. While life by definition can never offer any guarantees, it is always helpful to have information available for those who seek it. It also seems to be of crucial importance to the brightest people being attracted into international service today.

This was not the case when we entered the Foreign Service. The prevailing philosophy then was that children adapted and adjusted, just like spouses and employees. If they didn't, no one wanted to know or hear about it. Some parents -- as we did -- saw a wonderful chance to augment our children's education, language skills, and view of the world; other parents really didn't see the need to consider the children at all. Along side the legacy of growing up abroad is sometimes an uncomfortable legacy of parental guilt. Some parents watched as their children floundered in situations they had no control over, and had few, if any, resources to call upon to help them. That now seems to be changing somewhat.

As I write this I see our own children, now 26 and 23, right on target. Amy is about to marry a South African and plans to spend the following year in Africa with him while he completes doctoral research. She will attempt to learn Venda, which is his native language. Peggy, our younger daughter, soon leaves for Taiwan to spend a year teaching English to school-age children and perfect her own Chinese language skills which she has been building upon for eight years. Language, cross-cultural experiences and overseas living still preoccupy their 20s. By the time they are in their 30s they may be living in the United States or in other countries; I give it about a 50/50 chance! They both keep up very extensive correspondences with their friends from New Zealand and Africa. They both know they can live anywhere in the world. As rolling stones they have smoothed out nicely, but they can -- and do -- get caught in all kinds of unlikely places!

THE VOICES

THE MEN: Andy   **THE WOMEN:**   Andrea
                Craig   Barbara
                Michael   Christine
                Peter   Gail
                Rob   Julia
                Tony   Sally
                                                           Sarah

Andrea is still in her medical uniform when I arrive at the clinic after hours for our interview. Although a striking redhead, Andrea is soft-spoken, reserved and formal. She sits at her desk and starts her story slowly, sometimes painfully. She spent her childhood in Italy, Germany, Russia and India. The eldest child of five in a very close family, she had her own ready-made social unit until about the time she returned to the United States at 13, in time to take her high school education at a convent school in northern Virginia. That her parents were assigned to a remote overseas post just as she entered college turned out to be much harder for her than she -- or they -- thought it would be. Now 37, she is married and has two young children.

Andy is a man of quiet passion and engaging warmth. An early 60s activist, his actions spoke for him during his 20s and his writings spoke for him during his 30s. Now 40 he is a respected biographer and frequent contributor to a national political magazine. Andy grew up in five different countries in the Middle and Near East. His first educational experience at six was in an Arabic language school in East Jerusalem. A strong defender of Arab and Palestinian causes, he has been married for more than ten years to a woman of Jewish descent whom he met in college. They spent a year in Israel after they married. Andy was interviewed in front of a cozy fire in his three-story Victorian townhouse in downtown Washington, DC; his contemplation sometimes a contrast to the frequent sirens outside.

Barbara, at 29, is the youngest. Totally American in dress and appearance, she is eight months pregnant with her first child. We met at an appointed hour just outside the door to her row house in northern Virginia, where she was just returning from walking the dog. Married now three years, she and her husband, a foreign service officer, have already had two overseas postings. Easy, forthright and fluid, she reflects her parents' mid-Western origins. As a last, late child, Barbara was born in Pakistan and lived in eight countries on four continents before coming to the United States at 18 to go to college. She was brought up very differently from her three older brothers whose overseas experience was limited to Pakistan.

Christine, although slight, light in coloring and very feminine, gives the impression of someone who is steely strong when she needs to be. She is a woman just beginning to want to be in touch with her overseas childhood. After a period of wanting to forget her mobile past and uprootings -- born in Hong Kong, then to Kuala Lumpur, then to the United States for three years, then to Cambodia, Pakistan and finally Korea -- she now, at 30, seems in the process of trying to capture it, remember it, figure it out. She is a member of Global Nomads International and contacted me about an interview, but then seemed to pull back, wary of what such a thing might reveal. Christine is a talented musician, although her job in a local law office helps pay the bills.

Craig's first nine years were spent in a Philadelphia suburb, close to grandparents and lifelong friends. In the following nine years he lived in The Philippines, Morocco, Cambodia, Hong Kong, Bolivia and Brazil. When he returned to the Washington, DC, area for his last year in high school, he said the transition was difficult, to say the least. A compact, handsome and well-groomed man, Craig came to our Washington Capitol Hill townhouse for an interview before work one morning. At 42, Craig is a private person, a man who is comfortable in his own company. Although married more than ten years, his wife lives in New York during the week. Craig's professional life has been checkered with mobility, both overseas and within the United States. Now very content with his lifestyle and career, he is about to move overseas once again.

Gail's top floor skylighted condominium is filled with the memorabilia of her childhood years in India, Germany, and Ghana plus her Peace Corps stint in Zaire. There are innumerable photos of friends and family on the tables and walls. Like Gail herself, the surroundings are light, airy and expressive. Gail's ten year old daughter is patient about me taking her up mother's time for an interview. She and an unnamed orange cat wander in and out of the open plan living areas unselfconsciously. Gail, just 40, is a divorced single parent, although she shares custody with her former husband. Gail would like to work overseas again, but for now she has what she calls the perfect career for someone like her -- a top administrator at a private international school in Washington, DC.

Julia, 42, met me at the polished door to her elegant Boston Back Bay townhouse. She is a tall, slender, dark-eyed woman, with elegantly groomed long salt and pepper hair twisted into a bun. A loving corgi puppy hangs on her heels. The trimness of her appearance goes with the clean colors and lines of her house and furnishings. Half Jewish, her childhood experiences in war-torn Eastern Europe and newly independent India left her with stark memories of the cultures, deprivations and the importance of religious heritage. Married now ten years, she has grown step-children. She is a successful career woman working in a national public policy organization.

Michael was interviewed in his second floor office at the U.S. Trade Commission in Washington, DC. Clearly a happy man, pleased with his career, a relatively new and second marriage, looking forward to buying a home and having a family, he looked back on his roots with introspection and warmth. At 38 he is identifying what is important to him, and having stability definitely is important. He knows this because he spent several years as a Foreign Service Officer before taking his present position. Now he can travel, but he can come home too. His childhood was split between Europe and India; he lived in four different countries before he started college in the United States. This includes a last year of high school in a boarding school in Europe.

Peter is a missionary kid, for many years an only child of loving, doting parents. Peter's childhood was mainly spent in Korea but he had one year in England, where he boarded with a British family and attended a local cathedral school. His high school years were spent at a small, remote abbey his father created in the mountainous regions of Korea and where his parents still live. His formal schooling was through an American correspondence program. Peter's father was the son of a missionary to China. At 42 Peter is a large, warm, comfortable, yet brooding man, given to writing poetry and finding his own way theologically. He and his wife of ten years and their three children live in a century home in rural Connecticut which functions from time to time as a sanctuary. The day of our interview it was bathed in spring sunlight and strong colors. The comfortable kitchen was filled with children, dogs, cats, boarders and late breakfast aromas. Very settled from the outside, one of Peter's reoccurring themes during our interview was his restlessness.

Rob, father of four, homeowner and husband of ten years to his high school sweetheart from the large U.S. Department of Defense high school in London, still says he feels restless. Born in Japan, Rob lived in Tokyo, Tel Aviv, Cyprus and Rome before his first childhood stint in the United States. His six years in London, from ages 12 to 18, were a real high-point in his life. When I met him in Nordstrom's Department Store, he was between careers, caught between his resignation as business manager from a successful periodical and the start-up of his own company, which was caught by an unexpected recession. At 41 he is affable and athletic in a soft, comfortable way. Although still uncertain about his professional future, he is optimistic and accepting.

Sally's mother asked her my interview questions during one of her trips home to Michigan. Straight forward and clear in her thinking, echoing the professional technical editor that she is, Sally seems able to balance both the pain and the pleasure she had from her childhood years in England and Mexico. In England she went to local schools and found herself to be constantly the "only" American; she finished her secondary schooling in Mexico at a large international school. Now 30, she is just feeling settled after many years of restlessness and mobility during her 20s. She and her husband of two years recently bought a home in California and are looking forward to starting a family eventually. It appears from the interview that Sally has worked through her father's alcoholism and subsequent death.

Sarah is, at 40, strikingly classic Roman in appearance in spite of her denim jeans and sporty all-American demeanor. After a childhood spent in Holland, Sierra Leone, Switzerland (where she attended a boarding school), and Morocco, she entered the Peace Corps and went to Togo shortly after her graduation from college. She met her husband in Togo. His father was in the military when he was growing up, so he shares Sarah's mobility. He is now a lawyer. Sarah is a writer and researcher in archaeology, currently living in Alexandria, Virginia.

Tony, Sarah's younger brother, also lived in Holland, Sierra Leone, Switzerland and Morocco before entering an American boarding school for his last three years of high school. At 37 he is a Californian by nature and choice, open and full of good humor. He has his life just as he wants it -- both settled and international.   He works for a large multinational company that requires him to travel to Europe several times a year. He has lived in California since he entered university there in 1976. He is single.

CHAPTER ONE

CULTURE SHOCK:
LEARNING TO BE AMERICAN, QUICK!

Introduction

The notion that children raised globally will eventually "reenter" their own culture is a serious misconception. They can't really "reenter" what they've never truly entered -- at least not in the way their native born and raised parents can and think their children can. So right away there is this big difference in how parents and children experience the process. Children have to learn about their home cultures in the same way they've learned about other new cultures. But this time they don't have the benefit of being the different ones, the foreigners. This time there is no place for them to hide, and their peers can be unforgiving.

For example, there is no ready, comprehensible excuse for picking up the softball bat at the wrong end as one unfortunate boy did during his first year in an American elementary school. There is no clear and easy way for these so-called hidden immigrant children to communicate to their peers why it is they don't understand the current slang or get other common cultural signals. And, there is always that ubiquitous question dogging them: "Where are you from?"

Usually these children don't even realize themselves what it is that's missing. After all, they've always identified themselves as being from that "home" culture, as having a certain amount of understanding about it. They've often been there on extended home leaves, they have relatives -- aunts, uncles, cousins, grandparents -- who don't view them as strange. Very likely they have come from overseas schools where they have been immersed in what they thought was

American culture. Why is it then that they often describe their "homecoming" as like "coming from outer space?" They wouldn't think of using that analogy anywhere else in the world. That's because overseas they have a clear idea of their own identity: they are the foreigners. When they lose that "at home," they aren't sure anymore who they are!

Parents think they give their children the tools to survive in their own cultures as a matter of course, but parents of children growing up overseas have also made adaptations along the way to living outside their own countries. They are not "regular" members of their own culture either, by definition. They know this all too well after feeling the affects of their own "reentry." Parental knowledge about the culture can also become arrested while they are overseas. They are more likely than the ones who stayed "home" to reflect the values of their own generation, rather than evolving generations. This may be why so many children brought up overseas are caught in a time warp. They report feeling "out of it" within their own generation. They often feel uncomfortable with the morals and ethical choices being made by their peers. In effect, they are like cultural Rip Van Winkles.

Yet by any standard these same children tend to seem older, wiser, more sophisticated and worldly than their less internationally mobile peers. They often complain about the immature behavior they see in American schools and colleges. As consummate observers, they tend to stay on the sidelines, watching instead of joining in. For this reason their peers often see them as aloof and judgmental.

So do they go along with the crowd for the sake of popularity, to be like the others, or do they risk popularity to save their integrity? They want to fit in, they have "adapted" to situations all their lives; but at the same time, they are not certain they want to buy into their own cultural ethic except as an identifying handle overseas. They report being uncertain whether they actually do want to belong, at least if belonging means they have to invalidate the only past they know.

On arrival they seem to want a bit of both -- to be seen as "regular" while at the same time rejecting   that   label   for themselves. As they work it out, it is often described as "the worst time of my life." Only one of the voices described her entry into college as the best time of her life. In her case, this was because she was already accepted as and expected to be "different." She didn't have to pretend to be something other than what she was already.

It will be interesting to see how the more recent and increasing number of internationally mobile children from cross-cultural marriages handles similar entry into American culture. These are children who have been raised in two distinct traditions instead of one and have been raised in places outside either of those two cultures. Their signals have been even more muddled, more mixed, more complicated. Yet, on the other hand, these individuals may have the advantage of seeming different to their peers in either of their home cultures. They may more easily retain their tag as the foreigner and thus not be expected to conform to anything or even know all the rules.

Here is how some of the voices described their entry into America, their feelings and their frustrations. This is an area already well documented, but how do these memories and feelings carry over into adult lives and choices?

THE VOICES

Aliens and Their Alienation

Christine

The one reentry that particularly sticks in my mind was after the extended time we spent abroad, when we were away for six or seven years. That was after Pakistan. We came into Washington, DC, and I thought it was so clean and bright. I felt like a foreigner, and it was the strangest thing. I felt sort of happy that I could get a hamburger, I think. That's all I knew of American food. I didn't fit in. It was an odd feeling. I was shocked. I was going to start the eighth grade, and I truly felt like a foreigner.

It shocked me to read English signs, to see American people. I had seen them overseas, but not so many -- everywhere. I felt a sense of relief to be among people that were like me. I was happy about that. But the longer I was there the more I felt I didn't belong. I could tell I was different from my clothes, from my looks, probably from the way I couldn't relate to anybody about what was happening in their lives because my life was so different. I tried to fit in as best I could, but I always felt like an outsider. People didn't understand why I wore funny shoes, shirts with mirrors in them, embroidery.

There really wasn't anything familiar from when I was in the States before. I was too young. It was a different time of my life. I didn't have a sense of returning home.

Julia

... what I remember was coming back from Yugoslavia with long plain hair, gray woolen tights -- I had no clothes that weren't dull because that's all you could get in Yugoslavia. I wore shoes with little ankle socks. The other girls in the sixth grade all wore stockings. I felt like I'd come from Mars. It was desperately important for me to conform and not to be criticized by the other kids. There was a real battle, but by the end of about six months I'd managed to pretty well catch up.

Andrea

When I came back to the States as a teenager, I didn't feel like I had an identity. I was really shocked. I didn't know what I was supposed to be or what I was. We thought that we were American in India, but it was just so different. It was very hard to say what I was. I had to change that myself.

By far, the hardest transition for me was coming back into the United States and trying to get settled there. When you are moving from post to post overseas you are in this transient culture which all goes together. Other people are in the same situation. When you show up, people are going to be friendly to you because even though they may have some good friends, their friends may be leaving next month. They are much more open to you. Whereas when you come back to the States all of a sudden, people already have their friends. I started in this school where I thought everybody would be new, but of course that wasn't the case. Their whole culture was different.

When I returned -- as far as identification, I had none, right? I felt very American, but you see, it wasn't the "same" America. We come back, and the music is different because we were behind, and it was a whole different culture. We thought we were American, but we weren't. We were a mixture. We weren't really American at all. The worst part about it -- the thing I felt was the hardest -- was, as soon as you met somebody, they'd ask where you came from. To say you were in India ... "well, where are you from?" And then, they'd be kind of nonplused. What do you say at that point? Kids just treated us as if we didn't know anything. The things they wanted to talk about were TV shows or movies, music. I knew nothing about those things. Whenever I would try to start a conversation with anybody, and we'd start talking a little bit -- well, you know how people start trading stories -- and I'd try to give an example of something that was similar and I'd always start out with "When I was in Russia; When I was in India" because that was my whole experience, my frame of reference. The only place where things happened to me were these other places, because I'd only been in the U.S. a short time. Then, that would throw a wrench into the whole conversation. It would just stop everything. They would react with "you were?" or "where else were you?" It was very hard to make friends.

Tony

After my years in Kenitra and Tangier, I felt much more grown-up than my peers at Deerfield. In Tangier we had lived in a hotel and pretty much organized ourselves. I was aware of all kinds of things -- hashish, the large and active gay community. There was a sense of mystery in Tangier. I had all kinds of autonomy there -- contrast that to Deerfield with its serious rules.

Barbara

Kids don't know, they just reflect the environment that they're in. I didn't know anything bad -- I didn't know anything about drugs, until it hit me when we moved to Europe in my eighth grade. I didn't know about sex, drugs, lesbians, anything! My parents didn't sit down and talk to me about that. Kids only know what they see and how those things are reflected in the family.

Craig

When I came back to the States to live certainly I was no longer special, was no longer "an American." I was just one of the millions. That was a little difficult for me to accept. What I mean by being no longer American is that, yes I was American, but I was no longer an "American overseas," and being an American overseas is a lot different than being an American in America. They are special. The locals treated us as special, you had a select group of friends that you could feel very close with and identify with. I had none of that here. I was, essentially, adrift. I was in a place I didn't know -- didn't know the area, didn't know the geography, didn't know how to buy a hamburger. I adapted, I'm not saying that I didn't adapt, I did. But that doesn't mean I felt comfortable about it....

I tried to force friendships -- I needed to gain acceptance, real quickly. I made the wrong friends in some cases. Overseas everyone is on a time-clock, a rush to make friends and to fit in.... I discovered I had nothing in common with the kids at school. I would talk about overseas life, and they would look at me as if I'd just flown in on a magic carpet. After a while I just stopped talking about it because they just weren't very receptive. My identity felt very compromised -- they didn't know anything about these places. So, why bother? We had nothing in common and I always felt "on the outside, looking in." Just getting adjusted to teenage life here in America was very hard -- the music, the clothes, peer pressure was so strong that it was all a tremendous readjustment that I had to make. I didn't do well academically -- but then again, I was always an underachiever. I think a lot of it had to do with just having to deal with so much, with the pressure of trying to fit in. I did "time" in that high school and in college too. College was a four year "sentence." All of a sudden I was in a college with 30 thousand people. My high school in Bolivia had four people. College was horrible. I couldn't wait to get out -- I didn't even attend my graduation. My parents were back overseas then. They took an assignment to Vietnam in my second year of college. They'd left and I stayed behind. My sister was in Florida. I figured, who was going to come to my graduation? I had no interest in it, so I skipped it. On one hand I felt abandoned, on the other hand I felt totally free. It was a kind of dual-edged sword.

Rob

In 1968 -- that's when I returned to the States -- a lot of things were happening in '68. If you had to return to the States to live permanently for the first time, it was a tough time to do it. First Martin Luther King, then Bobby Kennedy were assassinated, the Tet offensive and the race riots in Chicago, Washington was burning, there was a drug revolution taking place here, and all I wanted at the time I came back was a Twinkie and a Coca Cola. And yet I was bombarded by all these different things that were happening. I remember getting off the ship -- we came back on the *SS United States* -- in New York and waiting for our car to be unloaded from the ship. My mother, father, and younger sister were with me. We got into the car, drove through the Holland Tunnel and out of New York heading south toward Washington. I was unhappy; I was melancholy. I enjoyed England -- I was 17 but would turn 18 in September. There was one little incident that happened on the highway going out which reminded me that I was in a little different society. In fact two things happened on that trip that were symbolic to me. We got to the toll booths entering the New Jersey Turnpike and right next to me a guy got out of a car and started running up a hill. Right behind him was a policeman firing in the air. Already guns going off. He wasn't firing at him, but this is it, we're here! It was probably a stolen car or something. That was the first law enforcement, Wyatt Earp type thing, I'd ever seen.   And then down the road I started watching the trucks -- the trucks on the highway were big and in England the trucks were much smaller. I can remember going like this (flashing the V symbol for peace) and

I can remember him giving me the "bird." I thought to myself, that's ridiculous. This means "peace" -- why wouldn't someone want peace? Those two symbols, those two gestures, really didn't ... I really didn't interpret it until a little while later. The truckers were part of the tattoo, flag-waving, redneck American culture, guns-for-hire generation. And I had offered them peace, love -- I had just come from the "love" generation where the Beatles and others were saying "all you need is love."

We came back to Washington and stayed with my brother before we found temporary quarters. I can remember spending at least four weeks in the basement of his house watching reruns of "I Love Lucy" and "Leave It to Beaver" -- things I'd never seen. I was sort of catching up on American television. But I was also very unhappy I wasn't in England.

Sarah

When I got to Bradford Junior College I was considered a foreign student. I remember that when I went to a meeting where they explained Halloween I thought I'd better tell them I really don't belong there! Like my brother, I was on shaky ground because I'd never seen our new home in Curacao, didn't feel I had a base, a place of my own to go to. Although I don't think this bothered me as much as it did my brother. But it was the first time I felt different. Maybe because of a loss of status, we'd had so much freedom in Tangier and here I was just a nobody, an anybody.

Sally

Those reentry years were not great years in my life; I pretty much wanted to be somewhere else but I really didn't know where I wanted to be. At the time, I really missed my boyfriend who was in Massachusetts. I knew it wasn't feasible for me to go back to Mexico because I didn't want to go to a Mexican university, I didn't want to live in Mexico. All my friends were sort of scattered over the States. There was really no other place for me to be. So it was difficult. My first year was difficult.

Peter

... there were situations where I was just like a bull in a china shop. I was just totally unaware. I missed the social cues. But at the same time, I had spent all that time with Americans in Korea, visiting friends military and missionary, so I thought I was completely American. But I was American with a difference. I knew I wasn't Korean, but I was completely comfortable in Korea. Seoul is the city where I am still the most comfortable -- of any city in the world. And I love Korea. But I always knew I wasn't Korean, and I always thought of myself as American. But then coming to the States ... I eventually began to understand that I wasn't quite the same as the other Americans. But it took me a while to see that.

I never felt a trauma during reentry, but what I experienced was that over a long period of time I didn't understand various things and I didn't know that I didn't understand them. That's why it took so long, I guess. ... those were some of the things my wife pointed out to me and helped me with. Then when she went to Korea -- we'd been married a number of years at the time -- she learned more about me. As she ... reflected back on the things she was learning, then I began to see them too. There was probably a period of about ten years that I was learning to live, to really be in American culture. I'd say it probably took me about ten years. One of the reasons for the long length of time was because I wasn't aware of what I didn't know. Lots of things have eventually showed this to me. Some of the problems I had in Texas that I alluded to, those were cultural reentry kinds of things now that I think about it. Just not picking up on the clues, the cues. Not knowing. People having expectations of me that I just had no idea about. I was making some assumptions that were not grounded, but based on my own experience. In the process I really ended up stepping on some toes and hurting people's feelings. One situation I remember very clearly ... what happened was that the pastor of the Presbyterian church, who was my boss nominally, had not been holding a tight rein on me or anything. He sat me down toward the end of the first year and said, "I know you said earlier that maybe there was an opportunity for you to work in North Carolina. This may be the time to do it. If you decide to stay here, I know we could use you, but I'm going to have tighter control because of" ... this, this and this. And one of the things he mentioned was that the church's secretary, whose son had died in Vietnam a year or so before, had objected to some cavalier comment I had made about being a Conscientious Objector, or about being against the war. It had really hurt her deeply. I totally blew this. He pointed that out, and I was heart-broken to know that I had hurt her so deeply. I went and apologized and asked her forgiveness, and it worked out well. But I learned to do that, and it had to be pointed out to me.

Michael

I never really took a good look at colleges. I tended to think in terms of what are the good quality schools I should be applying to, rather than what kind of a school I wanted to go to. Maybe I didn't think enough about the type of school I wanted to go to because I was used to just moving and just going into the school that was there. I never really thought of it in terms of choice. But I applied to a range of small liberal arts colleges and eventually went to one in upstate New York. Had I to do it over again, I don't think I'd do that. I'd not have chosen someplace so small and isolated.

I remember feeling during my last couple of years in college that most of the people that I knew from the foreign service had finished school and I felt unusual, not that I stayed in college, but went all the way through. Particularly since my closest friends -- dating back to India -- seemed to come back to go to college in the States but then never finished college and never seemed to get it together in terms of career. I was always a little perplexed by that.

Andy

Then I got on a plane and went straight to Minnesota. The first year back in America was pretty tough. I hated answering the question `Where are you from?' I took the line saying I was from Oregon, until I got to know people better. I think the first year of college is always sort of difficult, particularly so when winter set in. I'd never seen a North American winter, except for a few in Washington. The snow arrived in October and it didn't leave until April. I went through a lot of depression and loneliness.

I said to my parents that I wanted to go to a small school. I applied to six, including the University of Oregon as a fail-safe. I got accepted to three and Carleton in Northfield, Minnesota, cost less money. I really didn't think about where it was. It was purely by chance.... Carleton had at the time a junior year abroad program in India at Poona. The faculty advisor for that program came through Bombay with a couple of Carleton students during my senior year. My parents had them over for dinner, so they encouraged me to add Carleton to the list of schools I was applying to.

My depression was caused by a combination of a whole lot of things. I was still in this relationship with this woman, who was the daughter of missionaries, and she was in Colorado. And I was writing letters to her three times a week. I was depressed about that. It was also the weather. Plus all my life I'd been in this expatriate community, which is a small little village -- a small town. People have the wrong idea, they say "You've lived in Cairo and Bombay and Jerusalem -- you're very cosmopolitan." In fact, I wasn't. I arrived on campus and I didn't know how to drive a car. I didn't

learn how to drive until I was 20, some summer two or three years
later.   Cars were banned at Carleton anyway, so there was no
problem, but everyone I knew could drive a car.   I didn't know how
to deal with the long distance   operator so I could make a long
distance phone call -- I'd never done that before.   Also, in the
expatriate community you are protected because it's so small.   Like
buying groceries -- you buy them in the commissary, or they come
to your door or there are servants.   At mission school I was fed.   I
felt very awkward about going down to the grocery store in
Northfield and buying anything.   It was like dealing with strangers.
I'd never had to deal with strangers, except as an expatriate.   When
you're the foreigner, you're the observer, you're exempt from all
those rules.   In Cairo or in Bombay I went around by myself, and I
walked into restaurants and ordered meals by myself, but I was the
different one.   Yes, you're sort of "on stage."   People stare at you
and that sort of thing.   Then suddenly in Northfield I realized no one
knew who I was.   In Bombay or Cairo, everybody knew who I was
-- some American.   They didn't know that I was not really an
American -- that I was an expatriate.   And if I tried to explain it to
them, they would have said "say what?"   So I think for a while I sort
of shrank into my room.   I had two other roommates.   One had
grown up in Silver Spring and was very quiet, retiring, unassuming.
The other guy was more of an extrovert and more fun to be around.
I told them my stories, and where I came from or where I didn't
come from, but there wasn't a whole lot in common.   They weren't
politically active.   It took me a while to learn how to make phone
calls, to sort of feel comfortable around Americans.   And the
following year I got out of there!

Weighing the Choices -- Evolving into Ourselves

<u>Barbara</u>

After two years in Africa I really wanted ... my parents told me about the Oslo American School and how there were dances and boys, music. This suddenly seemed so exotic to me. I hadn't had any friends for two years that were my age. I couldn't believe it. I never thought about any of those other things I might miss. On the one hand I really missed Africa because I was wild and free there, and it was great having my mom as a teacher. I really missed Africa in retrospect. But I was eager to meet people my age and go to dances, and things like that.

But Norway and that school were really repressive. First of all, I was a civilian. I wasn't with the embassy, I wasn't with the military. And secondly, I was really "touchy-feely" because that's what I'd learned from my friends in Bukoba, the people of the Haya tribe. My best friends were the Luwaha Bruhas that lived across the way. There were eight kids in that family. The Africans are very "touchy-feely;" I mean you hold hands with girls, put your arms around each other, give each other hugs and kisses. It's no big deal. Here I was now in eighth grade in an American school and I was "touchy-feely" and they -- kids are cruel -- started calling me a lesbian. I didn't even know what a lesbian was. One kid in particular started this thing, so by the time I left, people didn't even know my first name, they just called me "Lessie" -- or a lot of people did. So that's where I became the champion of the underdog. Ever since that experience I haven't been "touchy-feely;" I won't touch anybody in public. It was just because kids are cruel.

I was strange and they couldn't figure me out. And I thought they were strange. Boys and girls were making out in the hallways, the military girls in particular were really into sex. Everyone I talked to seemed to have had sex already. So I hated Norway and I also hated the winters there.

The kids in my school in Riyadh were almost all government dependents. There were some kids from oil families. The kids in Saudi were so much better. These kids had traveled, they had been in diplomatic circles, they had interests; I don't think any of them had had sex before. It was like I was finally brought back to normal. I had friends and acceptance. I wasn't so close or part of a crowd, but it was a lot easier than Norway. It may be too because I was learning how I should react to these people. When you are taken out for two years, you're basically just a wild bird. Then if you are put in a very repressive social atmosphere, like an American high school, it can be really hard. It takes a lot of learning about what you say and what you don't, what is accepted and not accepted. I had learned African signals, which are totally different from American, and totally different than British, and British is totally different than American.

I guess I was pretty prudish, but I also thought most American kids were pretty stupid, starting from when I was in Oslo to Saudi Arabia and England. I was in high school in all those places and I really did feel that. The military girls were already having sex and smoking. I thought that was just ridiculous. In Saudi it was similar. A lot of the kids were from military or oil families. It was the same sort of feeling. There weren't shared values.

My parents weren't religious, and I'm not religious, so it wasn't because I went to church every week that I felt this way, I just felt it was wrong to do those things. In London, I wasn't in the "popular" group either because there the kids were very wealthy and they had a lot of drug problems.

It was really funny, especially in London, I didn't feel American. At one point I even argued with my father that I didn't want to go back to America for college. What I'd seen there frightened me. We lived for eight months in Reston, Virginia, before we went to London and I got to know -- you know Reston is a planned community and there are swimming pools and tennis courts and stuff -- some of the teenagers about my age at the swimming pool. They took me to their July 4th party and again it was the same thing -- people were smoking pot or using cocaine. The big thing was when they were going to get their drivers' license and get a car, they were already doing things with guys that I didn't think were appropriate, and here I was talking about the "geopolitical ramifications of the war in Cyprus." They thought I was boasting when I'd say "when I was in Cyprus I did this" or "when I was in such and such I did that." I wasn't boasting. They thought I was a snob because I wouldn't try a lot of the things they did. My father had a choice between going to work on a dam site with the US Geological Service near Las Vegas or going to London. And I can remember him sitting me down and saying, "What would you like? You've been here for six months, do you like it here?" I said, "Daddy, if we stay here, I'll become an addict -- this place is just awful!" You couldn't walk anywhere and I didn't want to learn how to drive. I didn't like the Americans I met -- I didn't think they were very smart. The kids my age didn't know anything about the outside world -- nothing! That really offended me.

When we went to London, my father said he'd pay for me to go to university, whichever college I wanted to go to in America. But you have to send in applications. I said I didn't want to go to America. At that time I had taken on a more British outlook. I used to march in anti-American missile parades, my best friend was British, my other friend was from Venezuela. I didn't dress like an American, didn't eat like an American, didn't talk like an American. I didn't want anything to do with it. I thought if I have to go to university and be in with the same sort of closed, provincial Americans, I would just be so unhappy. But my father said, "No, you have to go. You have to learn what it's like to be in America and you've got the wrong ideas about it. Not everyone is like that, you'll find your niche."

And it was the best thing because I went to Beloit College and I had a blast. When I looked to see where I wanted to go, everybody I knew from school was going to these East coast schools -- Harvard, Yale and Tufts and stuff. I didn't want to go there because I didn't like half those kids anyway. I knew Wisconsin, and I knew Illinois from my brothers, so I applied to both the Universities of Illinois and Wisconsin, and also a few private colleges. My father said I might be happier in a smaller college because a large school might be too big of a shock for me. I was accepted at all the schools, but the first college that accepted me was Beloit, so I went to Beloit.

My experience at college was really wonderful. My roommate wrote to me before I got to college. She was an intelligent biologist, and she was intellectual and smart. Beloit was great because a third of the student body was from Wisconsin and Illinois, a third was from other parts of the U.S. and a third was foreign. I was suddenly really popular. I had never been popular before! No one even liked me before, I guess just because I didn't approve of the things they did. Word spread on campus that there was this woman who had lived overseas all her life, and I was real wacky and interesting and "They should meet me." Everybody I met my first and second semester said, "Oh, (so) you're Barbara...." It really was wonderful. They were so accepting and so interested in the world. It was a great atmosphere to be in. Everything went well at Beloit. I had always been different, and I always refused to change.

Julia

... but I do remember this really serious sense of not being able to be who I really was. I think that's one thing that's fairly common among foreign service kids. In fact, I still have these battles and usually just revert to a "I'd rather not talk about it" stance. Also I found when I was in college sometimes people would be attracted to me for the stories I could tell and not for who I (was).

Gail

I do remember a lot about logistical issues and being in different schools and the stuff that went along with that. There are some things that are very clear emotionally, like going from seventh grade in Ghana, where, when I left I had my hair in a little ponytail and I was wearing anklet socks and little dresses that tied in the back, to eighth grade at Munich American High School, which is an Army high school. It was just unbelievable. They were wearing white lipstick, straight skirts and ironing their hair. They thought I was in fourth grade. I dressed like I was in fourth grade, but I was in eighth grade! I felt like I was in fourth grade for about two months; it was probably the fastest recovery job that anyone has ever done. I became "cool" almost overnight. It took a tremendous toll on me emotionally. It was just a terrible, terrible year. For that reason I remember having very bad memories of that high school and that whole experience, and those kids and how they treated me. I think it was partly because it was the worst possible time in my life for such a move. I was in two different countries with two different sets of values within the two schools. One was an international school and one was an Army high school, and much more like an American public school.

The kids at the Army high school were extremely "fast." I wasn't sure how to deal with that -- I hadn't run into that before. They seemed to have no sympathy at all for my position. I was just the weirdo. Luckily another girl came along who was also a weirdo because she came from a Catholic school in Paris. She had anklets but was slightly "cooler" than I was. I remember how hurt I was later because she also evolved, but part of her evolution was to deny me. We had been identified together earlier. As soon as she evolved into a "cool person," part of being a cool person was to slough me off. That happened for a while, and then eventually ... we're still friends today. We've been friends ever since.

Just the other day, my sister and I were riding home from Middleburg where our parents live and talking about the Munich American High School. She arrived in fifth grade and we just laughed hysterically when we thought about some of the things that had happened to us, and the adjustments we've had to make.... We were so used to this little enclave of Americans who fit within a certain definition in terms of the embassy and AID and those groups. These Army kids were so different. Their teachers were different, their parents were different. It was much more representative of real life, but it was representative of a totally different part of life than we'd ever been exposed to before.

I did hold to my own values -- pretty much so. I had to examine my own values pretty quickly and find out what they consisted of and make some adjustments. I guess that was the first time I started to have deeply held convictions about things and values and rights and stuff like that. I had to develop them. I remember having an argument with my father once. He was saying, "why don't you carry a knapsack to school with your books? It seems so much more convenient than your book bag, which you have to carry in your hand." And I had to say, "But no one else carries a knapsack." "But," he said, "why do you have to do what everybody else does?" And I said, "but you don't understand. I need to feel like I do what everybody does before I can do something different." That was a typical adolescent kind of response. I was working out all these things for myself in a very ethical kind of way because I was forced into this maelstrom of conflicting ideas about what it meant to be a young woman. Certain things -- like my mother wouldn't let me shave my legs and boys were making comments about it. My parents were more conservative obviously, although they adjusted quickly too. It took me a long time to get permission to wear stockings. Everybody else had been wearing stockings for a couple of years. Things like that were really hard, because my family's values came up against the culture's values. There weren't any real reasons for them to do that.... I was the eldest too. My sister had absolutely different experiences.

I hadn't had any real college counseling. I wasn't paying attention to suggestions that my parents say that they did make. I ended up at my mother's small college in the middle of Illinois. I had applied for early admission. It was my way of making a link and having something definite to hold on to that took me through that last year in India.

So I appear at this college in Illinois wearing Indian clothes and it was a total disaster. My roommate ... her father was in the oil business in Colombia. She also freaked out in her freshman year and turned into a hippy in about a week. It was also traumatic to find that although I thought I would like being an American, and thought that I was American, I found most of the things like homecoming and football games really stupid, ritualistic, and I didn't like any of it. I became clinically depressed when I was in college. That first year I had thoughts of suicide. I didn't have any capability to handle that, I didn't recognize it. It's since become apparent to me that it's something I'm subject to.... It's just something about my body that will come up in times of great stress.

But I was just lost! I was ten thousand miles away from my parents. I'd never ... I'd been so protected; "can't go to movies on Sundays because it's the day before school and a church day; and you don't go to parties past 12 o'clock at night." I'd always been very carefully taken care of, and then here I am ten thousand miles away and asked to take care of myself with absolutely no guidance and nobody to help me do it. I think that was a recipe for disaster, and I think that's how it happened to a lot of us.... There was no preparation and no expectation that we wouldn't fit in. When we came to the States it was always for home leave and everybody was so glad to see us -- presents, parties, relatives, fun. And it wasn't like that once you got here and had to live here. That was really quite unexpected.

I found out that all of my friends were upper-classmen from Massachusetts and New York and Connecticut. So I decided I'd better do something about that. I took the Barren's Guide to Colleges and looked for small, unusual colleges. I give myself credit because I'd never done a damn thing on my own before that.

I got accepted at four different colleges and ended up going to Bard in my second year. So I arrive in my Indian clothes once again -- to give it another try -- and everyone else is wearing Indian clothes too! But for different reasons. That was just wonderful; it was the perfect place for me. It was perfect because everybody there was a rabid individualist. Even if they didn't have my background, which only one other guy had, they were disdainful of each other completely because everybody was an individual. You can't be too friendly to anybody if you're an "individual;" but everybody was tolerated. It was really an amazing place. I don't know how, but it works, year after year.

Peter

When I was in North Carolina the second year of my alternate service, starting to think about college, I read an interview in Psychology Today with the president of Sarah Lawrence College about his ideas for the college. Right then I decided, that's where I wanted to go. All that I knew was that Sarah Lawrence was a girls' school. But I didn't care because I had very strong views about education, and again, these were ideas I had learned from my father and they weren't traditional. Sarah Lawrence was a non-graded system, no examinations, independent study -- a lot of radical kinds of things.... There was no clue in the article that men were there, but I thought, "That's where I want to go. That's it, there's no question about it!" Sarah Lawrence ended up accepting me and offering the best financial aid package of any of the schools I had applied to. I had absolutely no money. My parents had taken vows of poverty -- they had nothing to give me. I didn't have a penny to my name, but I didn't let that stop me. I ended up going to one of the most expensive schools in the country. So that's how I ended up at Sarah Lawrence. They had started admitting men three years before I applied. It was a four year experimental period, and I was at the tail-end of that four-year period. While I was there, during my freshmen year, they had a debate among the student body about whether to go forward.... One thing that struck me when I went there ... I went to school because I wanted to go to school and I wanted to learn.

When I got there, there were so many kids -- 16 and 17-year olds -- who were there simply because their parents were paying for them to go to college. What a waste! To me it was wonderful. Here I was, being housed, fed, cared for, and all I had to do was study -- things that I wanted to study, things I was interested in. Other kids didn't like that at all. But during this meeting, I was getting more and more disgusted with the kinds of comments people were making. They just didn't seem to address the issue of education at all. So I finally got a hold of the microphone and said, "When I found out about this school, this was what I wanted, this is where I wanted to go." I said I had come to this school because of its academic program. I read about it in an interview with the president, and I didn't know who went -- whether it was a coed school or just a women's school -- but I didn't care. It had the kind of program I wanted and I felt I would break down the doors to get in. And that was really the way I felt. Anyway, that little speech had a strong effect on a lot of people. I respected the school, and I felt a lot of the kids didn't respect the school -- they didn't know what they had. I treasured what was there.

Those were excellent years for me. I enjoyed it and I learned a tremendous amount. I had no apparent need to go to college because during those years in Texas and North Carolina I was doing a lot of reading, meeting with people. I had the sense that I could educate myself. I didn't really need to go to college. I didn't need a degree for the sake of the degree. But after a while, I saw that it would be worth doing.

CHAPTER TWO

STAYING IN TOUCH WITH "WHO I WAS WHEN"

Introduction

As internationally mobile children enter their own home cultures they come to realize very rapidly how different they are from their peers. Then they begin to figure out how these differences can be both a handicap and a gift. One theme that keeps surfacing among all the voices is how important it is for them as individuals to retain a distance, a uniqueness, which, as they reflect on it, has become an integral part of their own identity. After all, they were the kids who dashed around Tokyo and Bombay in baseball caps and blue jeans, or the ones who played baseball on empty lots in Ouagadougou. They were also the ones who, when they came out to play on a communal playground in Cold-War Moscow, sent all the local kids running back into their apartments lest they or their families be reported by the numerous security guards for fraternizing with Americans.

If for most of their childhood they have been seen -- and in turn been conditioned to see themselves -- as outside the majority population because of their country of origin, language, racial group, cultural and religious backgrounds, it is not hard to see how they might come to feel comfortable in that role, and in fact, to seek out that role in later life. Yet overseas they are a special minority, a minority with privileges and not so many responsibilities to the foreign cultures in which they live -- at least not the kinds of responsibilities they would have experienced within their own culture. It is often an element of their childhood they forget until they come up against it head-on as adults overseas, living in situations without the privileges. Conversely, it is also why so many return to careers overseas where the privileges are maintained along with the comfortable status as "foreigner."

When internationally mobile children finally integrate into American culture as adults they find themselves in a balancing act. They have to learn enough to fit in, make friends and get on with their own lives, while at the same time revalidating their childhood and that legacy. They seem to do this through work, study and travel abroad, keeping contact with past friends, seeking out photographic and material icons of their past, and rather willfully asserting their need to be "different."

THE VOICES

Early Lessons -- How We Came to Know We Were Different

Rob

All our relatives were in St. Louis. I'll never forget them coming to greet us at the station in St. Louis and when I got off the train I didn't even say hello to my cousins, aunts and uncles. I ran up to this little black boy on the platform and started speaking Japanese to him. The little black boy was in a state of shock. Everyone was in hysterics -- here's this American little boy speaking Japanese. The look on this other little boy's face was one of astonishment. I don't know why I picked out this little black boy. I guess he was the first kid I saw that looked my age. There was no suggestion of a racial situation -- I was color blind. He was just a kid and I was a kid, and Japanese was the language I spoke with other kids.

<u>Andrea</u>

We lived in a compound in Moscow. We were in an apartment. It was a compound which was like a high-rise, a four-sided complex. On our side, from the first to the sixth floors, there were only diplomatic families. There were Russian families on the other three sides of the complex. They had a security guard. On the playground he'd report on all the comings and goings. There was a playground we would share with the Russian kids, but it was funny because they were afraid to play with us. If they did, their parents would get so mad at them because they would be scared the KGB would get on them. It wasn't that the KGB was hurting these kids, it was just that their parents were scared that they would get in trouble if the kids were associating with foreigners.... It was really tough because it was kind of a no-man's land as far as Russian and American children. I do remember playing down there one time with my friend and we were chewing gum. This bunch of Russian kids came up and said, "give us your gum." We were starting to get kind of intimidated -- we didn't want to give them our gum. The only gum we had was what was in our mouths. And they still wanted it. So, I spit mine out and stamped on it on the ground, in the dirt, and ran off. I don't know if they took it or not, maybe they did.

I remember having nightmares about people coming out of the walls and grabbing our family. One way that I know I was afraid, that was real, was that my father ... he was at the point where he was considered fluent in Russian and he would go out. They had some demonstrations against the United States while we were there and he would go out in the crowds and mingle with the people. I heard him telling stories about what it was like and this one guy saying to him, "Where'd you get your shoes?" And he'd have to say, "Oh, I had this friend and he brought them to me from England." And then, "Where'd you get your coat?" Maybe his looks and language could blend in, but there were things about him that weren't exactly right and in retrospect I can say he really wasn't in danger, because those demonstrations were really very controlled things. But I didn't realize that at the time.

Barbara

We went to Nairobi, Kenya, before we went to Bukoba, Tanzania. I didn't go to school in Nairobi because we would be ... two weeks in Nairobi, and then take a bush plane -- oh, those bush planes! -- from Nairobi to Kisumu, Misuma and Mwanza and then across to Bukoba; or we would drive from Bukoba around the southern part of Lake Victoria to the Serengeti National Park. It was awful -- I wanted to be a boy! I refused to wear a bra and I'd only buy these kinds of shirts that had dark embroidery over the front, and I cut my hair really short, and I wore safari clothes. I didn't want to become a lady. There's something wild and vibrant about East Africa.

Peter

There were some things about being different that I didn't like. For instance, as a little kid I hated it when the Koreans would stare at me -- this blue-eyed, blond haired kid. They would always stare. We would go some place in the car, and as soon as we would stop, they would just be at the windows of the car, pointing and trying to touch me, saying how pretty I was and cute. I hated all that. And I hated being waited on. I hated being made to feel like people needed to serve me.

I had some Korean friends as a little boy. We were just good friends -- kids in the neighborhood. And I liked that. We played together, but I didn't like being elevated. I was different than the other missionaries. Most of the other missionaries were Presbyterian or Methodist and we were Episcopalian, our mission was in England. It was the Anglican mission. We didn't live on a mission compound, whereas the other missionaries did. The military people all lived on the military compound. We were the only ones that I knew who didn't live on a compound -- we lived with Koreans around us.

I spoke more Korean than most of the other kids in the school. So these things always set me apart from the other Americans as well. So I've always been -- from the time I was seven -- different from almost everybody else. Different from the rest of the mission community, different from the Koreans.

Sally

I would say definitely I have felt myself to be a minority. It was probably more uncomfortable in England when I was a kid than it was when I was in Mexico during my high school years. In England I went to school with all English kids and I felt sort of the outsider, although I had a lot of friends. In Mexico I went to a school with mostly other Americans and felt much more at home there. In general too, Mexicans tended to like Americans and American things more than English people seemed to. I felt less hostility in Mexico than I did in England.

I've always thought of myself as different. In England I was the only American in my school and in Mexico I was different, but more of a collective different because there were more of us. But we stood out because we were light haired.

Getting Used to "Standing Out"

<u>Julia</u>

I remember stories from my friends in India who had moved, recounting stories about how some felt like big fish in a small pond, and then moving back to the States where there was a small house, no servants, not having the status of their dad's position. We were definitely aware of status issues at the International School but I don't think it affected our friendships. People treated me in certain ways because they knew my dad was senior and close to the ambassador. It was such a small place everybody knew that. In the normal course of events you wouldn't even know what your classmates' fathers did for a living. It was irrelevant. I remember some of the parents of my friends were clearly on their best behavior when I was around. I remember the status issue not so much with my friends but when with their parents.

<u>Sally</u>

I remember this woman in my college dorm talking about some friend of hers who had just come back from some vacation in Europe, and this was supposed to be this wonderful thing. I thought to myself "hey, wait a minute -- I lived there." It seemed like a weird reaction. Like people who can afford a vacation in Europe are somehow better than people who have lived there....

I think I felt more of a loss of status when my parents moved back to the States, to be honest. We had lived in a really nice neighborhood in Mexico and we had rented a pretty big house. Then when they moved back to the States they moved into this little condominium, in this little boring town, and I thought ... I definitely felt a loss of status. I thought, why aren't we living in a nicer neighborhood? I guess I really wasn't happy when they left Mexico and what choices they made when they came back. But they did what they could afford to do. My dad retired and they had to adjust their living to their income. But to go from a vibrant metropolis like Mexico City to Rochester Hills was a big transition, and I was used to more excitement in my life.

Rob

I got an English taxi cab while I was in London -- bought it for 75 pounds. I was the only kid running around with a privately owned English taxi cab with a meter on it and (diplomatic) plates; I'd park anywhere I wanted. We'd put the Budweiser where the luggage goes and go out and party. It was a fun time. It was a good safe car and never went faster than 40 miles an hour. It was built like a tank. I'd go down to Leicester Square with 10 or 15 people in this darned thing. I dated my wife in this taxi and she would sit on the heater box right next to me. I couldn't be missed in that taxi. I think that it was the only taxi in London with an "L" learner's plate!

Accents -- Using Them, Losing Them

Sally

I picked up an English accent during the first two years of living in England and lost it for the most part on our first home leave. When we first came back on home leave everyone made a big fuss over the cute accent I had and would say, "Say something in English, Susie!" My shyness overtook me and I would get embarrassed when I was put on the spot like that. During that six-week period was when I lost my accent. I never again regained it, although it was not a conscious decision. I was only seven.

Rob

I think language has to affect the way you think. If you cap off childhood with living in England, where they measure every phrase and every word they speak, you get a sense of deliberation in how you capture a sentence, how you put it together. I think it does reflect how I speak. Some people that know I lived overseas are surprised that I have such a neutral accent. Why, after living in England for six years, didn't I come away with an English accent? When I was living there I sort of preserved my (American) accent because I didn't allow it to change. I didn't feel compelled to assimilate in that area. Whereas others developed a British inflection. I guess I felt strong enough to hang my neck out.

Gail

In terms of languages, what we learned was a whole bunch of different accents. When we went to India we came back speaking with British accents, and then we went to the United States and learned how to speak like Americans, and then we went to Ghana and learned pidgin English and acquired British accents again, and then we went back to an American high school in Munich and learned to speak like Americans again, then we went to India and learned to speak (with an Indian accent). We talked to each other all the time like that.... When we get together with friends from India we do a lot of that. It feels very familiar and good.

Trying to Go Back to Where I Think I Belong!

Andy

I came back and went to college at Carleton and then very much wanted to go back overseas again. Instead of doing a junior year abroad I applied to go as a sophomore. I got permission to go to Beirut, I wanted to go back to my roots and I had a choice of either Cairo or Beirut.

Gail

Immediately after college I went into the Peace Corps. It was only about a month later -- I couldn't wait to get back overseas. I was living in Ghana when the first Peace Corps Volunteers -- ever -- arrived in country, 1961 I think it was. I met a few of them and I was so inspired; it was the only.... Well I knew I wanted to be a nurse all my life, and I wanted to be in the Peace Corps all my life. I got older and I didn't become a nurse because you had to deal with math, and I thought I was bad at math. It turns out later, that wasn't true at all. So then I thought I had nothing to offer Peace Corps, so for a few years in there I thought I would have to abandon this. I started looking at emigrating to Australia. Then I finally realized Peace Corps was going to take people who were generalists and I could apply. I was really very, very happy to find that out.

Those were my only career choices: emigrating to Australia and finding work there or going into the Peace Corps. I didn't even consider staying in the United States. I think it was just desperation to get back overseas. I didn't want to feel like I was trapped in this country forever. That was really the motivation.

Then, of course, going back overseas by yourself in the Peace Corps is quite different from being with your parents in the "golden ghetto." That was where I experienced another one of my depressions. I think it was because I had very little company and certainly no sympathetic company or anyone who was even like me. I was teaching English in a Protestant mission about 90 kms outside of Kinshasa, Zaire.

Craig

Two weeks after I graduated from college I was in the Peace Corps, assigned to Afghanistan. I couldn't wait to get overseas again. I felt that was my niche, that's where I felt comfortable. I was assigned to Kabul, the capital, and was there not for years, but four weeks. I ended up getting very bad dysentery, and I was disillusioned with Afghanistan too. I wasn't particularly thrilled with what I saw.... It was more like being a local, living off the land. We didn't have a commissary -- it was overseas life from a very different perspective. We were thrown into it to a much larger extent. You could blow your whole salary by getting a hamburger at the American Club.... I wasn't really too sad to leave. I got very, very sick and came back -- but I didn't know where to come back to. Where do I come back?

I did come back to Washington and because ... I was interested in photography, I went to work for a national photographic chain, as a salesperson. I didn't think it was going to be a long-term thing. One thing led to another and they made me manager, and I did very well with them. I was really surprised. They sent me overseas. They had an operation in Tokyo. At that time it was a joint venture with a Japanese company and they were trying to see if they could make money selling stuff to overseas tourists. That was when the dollar was pretty strong. So I was with them for about five years; I was in Japan for maybe a year and a half altogether. I was also working part time for their export agent in Japan, writing English instruction books. I had a great time, I had a wonderful time. I loved it -- I was overseas again, I was special, I was an American who was treated as special. I was in my element. I had a Japanese girlfriend. But the dollar started to drop. We weren't making any money. I think I was getting a little homesick for the United States. I started thinking I'd better close this operation and start getting back....

Rob

I was very unhappy to leave London and did fly back the following Christmas.... I was there for three weeks. Then and there I realized it would never be the same. It was different. The fact that my parents weren't there, my home wasn't there -- I was on my own and vulnerable. I either had to make it on my own, or leave. I couldn't work there legally. Those who did, did it under the table. There was no opportunity for me.

Michael

... I remember when I was in college I said I never wanted to go into international work; I said I would never go into the Foreign Service. This was for a variety of reasons. I was hung up on the notion of not following in my father's footsteps. I was less interested in international politics and more interested in international economics -- better adapted to AID work, Work Bank interests -- and then I worked for the Peace Corps for a while here in Washington and the next thing I knew I'd joined the Foreign Service.

I remember the first time I went back to India. Before that time I had always wanted to go back, and I can remember other people saying to me "Don't think about going back because when you go back to a place, it is never the same as it was when you were there. It is always a disappointment." That was a constant thing I heard in later years when I was at the Peace Corps; volunteers were always talking about going back to their countries and the lore was always, "Don't do it." But I really wanted to go back to India. I can remember when I did, at about 20, 21 -- I had left there at 14 -- the last thing I ever expected was that when the plane landed and the doors opened the smell would come back over me as it just wafted through the air. It is something I never even thought about, much less remembered. It just smelled different, and I remember that smell fondly. That particular memory has always stuck with me. Then I took a cab into the town, and in a lot of ways it looked very different, but there were so many -- despite all the new buildings and hotels that had gone up -- ways it was still the same place I'd left.

I've always tried to find ways to get back to that area of the world within my career as well. I was Bangladesh desk officer for a while in the State Department and through that I got to travel back. I had other jobs as well, and even working in trade here, it is an area I remain interested in and I look for ways to return.

I would like to go back to Germany and Switzerland, but not in the same kind of way as India. I think part of it is because it wasn't as different an experience as India was. I wasn't there for as long a period, and not in my formative years. ... with India it is a gut thing. When I get back there, something of that country is still in me.

Sally

Sometimes I get worried that I'm almost losing my ability to feel comfortable in another country -- that the next time I go to another country it's going to feel real foreign and I'm going to have a harder time feeling comfortable because it's been so long since I've done it. But I hope that's not true.

Gail

I haven't really been able to afford to travel that much. But I had a very interesting experience two summers ago when my friend Gabrielle had some free tickets from her frequent flyer miles. She took me to Kenya with her. I hadn't been in Africa for many, many years -- not since I was in Zaire in 1975. I hadn't really been overseas to a third world country in years and years, since I went briefly to Mexico in 1978. So I thought, how much of this is left from my childhood? Is there anything left? Is there anything that was really in me, or was it just an experience? We touched down in that airport in Nairobi and I was right back home in five seconds! I knew that the taxi drivers were going to try and cheat me, and that we had to cut the baggage handler out from the herd to get one instead of 15 of them and make sure that this guy wasn't cheating you. Then to figure out how to get into town -- then the closeness of the atmosphere and the humidity, the hibiscus -- everything was just screaming, "You're home, you're home!" It was just so wonderful. I felt so glad because it was the first clue that I'd had -- and I had been worried that I didn't have this stuff anymore -- that it wasn't just a memory, that it really was part of me. This really confirmed it.

... we were out on safari, and all of a sudden this stuff would start coming out of my mouth which I didn't know I knew about these animals, about their habits and about how rock hyraxes are the closest relative to the elephant. Everybody looked at me like, "You're out of your mind. Where are you getting this information?" It was all stuff that I had learned from being on safaris before in East Africa and just stuff I accumulated; information that had been totally useless to me all the rest of my life and had never come out of hiding, stored in my brain all these years, and the minute the key was inserted, it all came out again. So there are all these little compartmentalized bits of knowledge that I never use in this country -- and never have the clues to open the flood gates and tap into that stuff. Yet under the right circumstances, obviously, it's right there.

Holding to the Touchstones

Michael

    I am a bit of a packrat about my things. I have all the little things I've picked up overseas and, wherever I go, those are going with me. I think my wife was kind of surprised when we first started going out to find how really established I was. She hadn't expected a single man to accumulate all that stuff. Every time I've moved -- I've moved a fair amount since I've been in the Washington area from one apartment to another -- I'm almost manic about unpacking. I get the boxes open and everything set up and in place immediately. I stay up all night until it's done. I don't like living with boxes. That must go back to my childhood. As soon as I can unpack all of my things, that's my stability. Those are the only things I've had and when they are all out, and I can see them, then I feel some kind of definition.

Gail

    Foreign service apartments are so interesting ... I know immediately when I am in a foreign service apartment. It's always so interesting to see what other people have because they always have artwork from different countries and crafts and things like that. You can always tell immediately where they've been posted. I've gotten interested in quilting lately. My baskets are from Bhutan, the quilt is a piece made by my friend from eighth grade in Munich. She gave it to me as a wedding present. I bought that vest in India when I was in high school. These things remind me who I am.

    I've thought about what one thing I would take if I had to leave my house in a hurry. I realize that the one thing I would take is my jewelry box and it's not because I have any jewelry that's of any value, but my jewelry is one of the things that sets me apart from other people and makes me feel different because my jewelry is from countries all over the world. It is really interesting jewelry. I can never imagine why people like to go into jewelry stores in this country because it's so boring and I can't see a single thing that I'd want to buy! But my jewelry box!

Sally

I can think of two things I would save if my house was burning. One would be my jewelry box because most of the jewelry I have has been given to me by other people and it has a lot of sentimental value. The other would be my photographs. I don't know how I could take them all out, but that would be a devastating loss for me. To lose the pictures ... my friendships are so important to me and that's what I have. I can't go back to England, I can't go back to Mexico. There's not really a place to go home to, so if I'm ever feeling homesick I have to look at my pictures. That's where it is now.

Barbara

... we dated for three years before we got married and during that time I think I really opened his eyes. He'd never had Pakistani curry for instance. In our family, when we get together for Thanksgiving, we have a Pakistani curry and lots of different ones. It's so hot that you're sweating even though it's 30° F outside and only 65° inside. The first time I had him over for dinner I made him the hottest Pakistani curry ever. I thought, well this is a test! He'd never had any hot food before in his life. And he loved it! His face got all red and we had to have lots of beer, but he loved it. To this day he insists we have it at least once or twice a month.

Christine

I got rid of most of my trappings of that other life, but I think it would be neat to have them now. It would remind me of who I was back then. But, I just didn't want anything to do with it, and now I regret it.

When I go to my parents I do have those things from my childhood. The things they have are touchstones. I feel good about going to them and seeing all these things. I wish I had kept some of the stuff that was given to me. I had a beautiful prayer rug that I didn't appreciate when I was younger. It went to the moths.

Asserting Our Distance

Gail

I grew up wanting to be different, and wanting to appear different. I'm not sure why -- I've never been able to tease that apart, but there are things about me that would set me apart in a way. I don't know if they are attitudes that have come out of having lived overseas or not. It's really hard to tell. I might have been that way anyway. But I have a definite need to be different from other people in the group -- as an adult. It may not be obvious in some ways, but when people get to know me they realize it's pretty true. I need to feel special, even if it's only apparent to me.

Peter

I've always been different. And I've always found pride in being different. Partly that's making the best of the situation, partly I think because I've always liked to stand out. I like to be alone a lot too. I spent a lot of time alone.

Barbara

I like being the "different one." Even in this culture I am different. My husband gets mad at me. He says, "You always say you don't want to be conventional.   You always use that word --

conventional." That's true, I don't want to be conventional. I don't want to be like any of the Americans I know. I want to be totally different. I am, whether I like it or not.... It's not that conventional is a bad word, it's just that -- I like to think I can go in and out of different segments of American society. I have a group of friends who are vegetarian and very politically correct, and a group who are extremely conservative and very wealthy, and then I have the misfits like me.... Then I have my professional friends. They live in the suburbs, they only eat quiche hot. And they are delightful. There are a lot of different facets.

Christine

Now I feel pretty American, but that's something I've been struggling with too because now I think I've lost all my foreign identity. I tried to adapt too much. I've noticed some of my friends have never really gotten over it. My friend in Arizona is making jewelry. It's probably what she wants to do. I sort of went the other way; I wanted a career, I wanted to make money, I wanted to, you know.... I sort of feel I'm getting beyond that now. My brother did that. He was in the corporate world for many years and all of a sudden he said, "I hate this and I'm going to teach rock climbing." He gave up everything and moved to West Virginia.... He's been there eight years, or so.... He's really happy....

I think my brothers were struggling with their identities. I think we all do, all the foreign service people. We're different, we've seen things that other people haven't. They can't possibly understand because they haven't been in that situation. I think that the knowledge that we have -- that they will never understand -- is sort of hard to bear. I, especially, have always wanted people to just sort of understand me, and not look at me as different. But.... Of course, people say, "Oh yeah, I can really relate" or "That's really interesting that you lived there." And then they go off and, it's like, "don't you understand? This is a big part of my life. Become more involved with me. Understand what I went through."

CHAPTER THREE

LIVING ON THE SURFACE

Introduction

All of us who raise children in foreign countries struggle between the need to make our children feel a part of and comfortable in their home cultures and giving them some understanding of the cultures in which they live. Sometimes we lean out too far in one direction along this cultural tightrope, sometimes too far in the other direction. We worry about whether our children will ever be able to fit in at home; sometimes we wonder if we will ever fit in again!

Expatriate families, taken as a unit, by definition live on the surface wherever they find themselves. They become observers, not participants. They can voice opinions, study political activities, help local people to make their lives better or worse, but in the end, one fact remains; they always leave. They know this from the day they arrive, and so do the people they meet along the way. While friendships may be maintained for lifetimes afterwards and visits can be arranged to and from, the fact remains that the expatriate and the landed are apart -- geographically, culturally. As an emotional self-protective mechanism we often draw a line between staying marginal to the culture and getting involved beyond our abilities to withdraw. It is insightful that out of the 13 voices only one mentioned missing anything about the physical landscape where they grew up. For the others, they didn't seem to take much notice of where they were living -- whether near the sea, in a desert, near mountains or in the tropics. It just didn't come up as a topic. Also, not one of the voices seems really attached to the geography where they find themselves living now.

One result of growing up this way is that children really don't get a chance to see their parents participating within their home culture in a way that is natural and normal. While they are overseas they are usually outside the local laws, they don't vote or hold strong political views, and they don't have the cultural continuity provided by other family members nearby. Sometimes children have heard their parents or other expatriates openly malign the local people. Families usually don't or can't participate in a religious community the way they might at home. They miss out on the usual rhythm of births, deaths, marriages and multi-generational get-togethers. So, if in their adulthood these children become marginal to their home culture, is it something they learned from their own expatriate family experience, or is it a result of really seeing themselves outside the mainstream of their own culture? Perhaps it is a bit of both.

The marginality certainly seems to be borne out by the voices; they are not joiners and are often most happy in their own company, they vote but otherwise are political observers, they are not blindly patriotic and in fact the notion of patriotism in any form bothers some a great deal, and they are often embarrassed by the staggering wealth and waste they see around them. They don't like being pinned down on that "where are you from?" question. They would rather skirt it to assume citizenship in a larger world rather than limit themselves to the locale in which they currently live.

Again, we hear the echoes of wanting to be different, to be separate -- of wanting to assert a status gained through years of experience and practice. We also hear echoes of not wanting to get too close, be too vulnerable, to any one place or any particular group of people; emotional investment that might not be sustainable because they know "things change."

THE VOICES

Learning to Go with the Flow

<u>Craig</u>

My friends overseas were, for the most part, American foreign service or military brats. They weren't particularly special, just average kids. We always knew that we would leave -- that was a given. You were always running to the airport saying goodbye to people. Everyone knew it was a two year gig, or a three year gig; some went on home leave and then came back. We were continually bouncing around. We knew that, and I think we would try to pack in as much during the period together as we possibly could.

<u>Rob</u>

As I was growing up I learned to seize each moment; almost an existential life. You are presented with lots of opportunities at different times of your life that you could take advantage of ... you had to take it all in. There's a point where you sort of sit back as an observer. You're on a ride, going with the flow. The suggestion is that rigidity has no place in your life, flexibility is the key word....

<u>Peter</u>

From the very beginning -- from the time I went to Korea -- there were so many different worlds intermixed in my life. They never got confused. Whoever I was with, I was with ... and I was with at their level.... But I think part of it may have been that I learned early on to adapt, so that wherever I happened to be, or whoever I happened to be with, I would be with them and like them. Then I'd go somewhere else and be someone else. But to me it was never a problem -- I never felt divided. It was all part of my world. It was just that my world was very varied. So wherever I'd be, that's who I would be for that period of time. Whether it be with Koreans traveling third class on the trains, whether it was staying with an American military family, or going to the movies with other missionary kids, or with adults at the seminary.

Sally

I think I identify with other Americans, but I identify better with Americans who have lived overseas. I don't have any trouble relating to people usually and I have all kinds of friends who have had all kinds of different experiences. Sometimes they've lived in one county of the same state their whole life and sometimes they've moved around a lot. Relating to people doesn't seem to be a problem for me.

Keeping Our Distance

Michael

Some of the people here at the office depend on the office for their friendships. The office is more than nine to five; it is a very important part of their lives. Whereas for me I get along with people, but there is a little bit of aloofness there. I don't get so involved in the parties, and I sort of tend to keep my social life separate from my professional life. I've never really attributed that to anything, but.... There is someone just leaving this office -- it's her last week here -- and she's been here about ten years. I was just talking to someone this morning about how hard it is for her to leave and how she's developed a lot of close friendships here and what a difficult thing this is for her to leave. I got to thinking, "I've been here five years and I don't think it would be that hard for me to just get up and move on."

I have more of a tendency to have a smaller number of closer friendships, outside of work. With the others at work, I get along with them very well, but I resist the emotional investment.

Sally

I hardly have any community involvement. Maybe there's a connection there.... We have friends that we do things with, but we aren't involved in any community type things.... I'm a joiner -- I love to be around people. I love to have friends, and I love to have parties. I'm a joiner but I'm not a "formal" type of a joiner, in terms of joining clubs, organizations and things like that. But I like to have a lot of friends and I like to cultivate friendships. I like to get together with groups of friends and do things.

Peter

I don't actively belong to any groups, other than the church. Really, I don't. From time to time I've been involved in one thing or another, but my life is really full. Between my secular career as a consultant, the church work and then the family and household, that's enough. I like to write, there is some writing I want to do in relation to the church -- training materials, theology. I have very little time for other kinds of organizations. I'm very politically conscious, politically aware, but not politically active other than just in conversation.

Rob

I'm active here with the kids' soccer.... But as far as being civic active, no, I'm not. I'm an armchair sort of person. I don't have a sense of efficacy. To be involved civically, it's never really interested me. Organizations seem to be used for the wrong reasons, or rather the people involved in them use them for the wrong reasons. They just become an arena to vent anger and frustration. And nothing good ever comes of it.... We have a strong sense of independence. There are a lot of Americans who don't want to join anything; people who won't move into a neighborhood because it has an association and they don't want to be associated.

Gail

One of the things I've learned about myself from Global Nomads is, while the director kept trying to get me to join, I asked myself, why is it I don't want to join? I finally realized I don't want to join anything! I don't want to join.... I'm just somebody who likes to have individual relationships, but I don't like being part of groups.

Craig

... I've always felt neutral about Washington, whereas other places I've either hated or loved; Washington I've never had a strong feeling about one way or the other. I don't hate it and I don't particularly love it. For someone like myself, it is actually one of the better places to be. It has so many transient people -- people are constantly in and out, it's very cosmopolitan. I feel more comfortable in Washington than I would, say, in New York, where I spent a lot of years. I feel New York is very provincial actually. Unless you are born and raised in New York, no way in the world would you feel comfortable there, I don't think.

Now that I'm in Alexandria, Virginia, I feel as though I'm "home" to a large degree. I feel I've come home. It's difficult when you are alone during the week to be involved. I don't think the Washington area is necessarily that "kind" of area -- people don't tend to get to know their neighbors the way they used to, anywhere. I think that's a choice. I think I'm a little reluctant to become too close. I have a dog, which keeps me busy. I do a lot of reading. I like a lot of time by myself. My pursuits are limited, I guess, in terms of physical activity. But that's my choice. I'm perfectly happy to stay home listening to the stereo, nobody bothering me, reading a good book, taking a walk.

I really don't have too many friends here. Most of my friends are at work, but they are not socializing friends. But I don't have a need for a lot of friends. My wife is not here during the week -- I'm pretty much of a home-body. But that's my decision. I just like a lot of time to be alone to do what I want to do. We know the difference between friends and acquaintances -- very much so. Even the friends that I've had since returning to the United States, there has always been a difference between me and them in terms of the overseas experience. You can never overcome that -- that's something that you have that's unique to you that they just can't fathom. It is always a part of your life unless they share that same background. You certainly can like people, but that's such a big part of your life that you can't share with somebody else -- there is always that gap.

Andy

Washington is a very odd sort of America. Particularly in D.C. As a white male, living in a city that is virtually segregated, where I could never expect to have real influence over political decision making in this town, or run for political office or any of that, I'm like the expatriate again -- the observer -- living right there on the surface, but not responsible. All my friends are other observers -- other journalists or people who work as congressional aides or, like my wife, working in the development business.

Our World Is Larger Than Just One Nation

Barbara

Sometimes when I'm overseas I'm so proud to be an American, and then sometimes -- more often than not -- I feel more like a citizen of the world than a citizen of America. That isn't necessarily good because you don't have an allegiance. But often I just don't feel American for many reasons.

Gail

I have a real sense of dismay about nationalism and patriotism. I hate those things. I hate all this stuff about flags and national anthems and loyalty oaths. That stuff really turns me off, and I don't know how much of that is part of my international upbringing, but it may be.... A friend of ours just got married last weekend and she grew up overseas. They were talking about how she was going to have ethnic food at her wedding and my father was saying, "Why is she having ethnic food at her wedding? She's not ethnic!" I reminded him that she had grown up overseas and she wasn't exactly American, those countries where she's lived are a part of what her ethnicity is. He didn't realize that because he didn't grow up overseas, he went overseas as an adult. For him, he was already a fully formed American. But to me, the American food would have been just as legitimate, but the ethnic food was a part of her own identity. That point was not understood by my father. I think it showed the difference between those of us who grew up overseas and those who went as adults.

... I saw my status in a negative sense mostly when I was overseas because I felt like we had so much and everyone around us always had so little. To me it was intensely embarrassing and a source of a great deal of sadness for me, particularly in India. I was extremely sensitive, I think, anyway by nature, but it was enhanced by the extremes that I saw around me. I remember when I was a little kid and I was still praying, my prayer was "Please God, give everybody everywhere everything they need." I had to include the animals, and I had to make sure this group was taken care of -- I couldn't afford to leave anybody out because everybody was part of my universe. It was a bit of a stress getting up to this point because I was so guilty about leaving this one out or that one out. It was really very difficult for me and only as an adult have I been able to put all that stuff into perspective and understand. But, it is still really painful for me to see the differences and feel like I'm not doing enough to take care of the homeless -- not volunteering to do this or whatever, and I think a lot of that comes directly out of that experience. There were so many contrasts. It's still somewhat unresolved. Even though I'm healthier about it mentally, because I've learned how to work through it and I couldn't survive unless I did, but it's still painful a lot of times to see things that way and feel that way.

Craig

When I got back from Afghanistan I went to a supermarket here in Maryland and saw all this food and I literally went into some kind of shock. Just seeing this abundance of food when I had just, within hours or days, come from a place people were literally starving to death. The contrast was so overwhelming. It really hit me. Here we are so rich and fat and spoiled. Over there they are fighting for a crumb of bread. I think Americans are spoiled.

Peter

I was never a part of the "anti-war" sentiment, although I was very sympathetic towards it. I felt I should fulfill my responsibility, do my alternate service; I didn't feel I was evading the draft. No running off to Canada. On the other hand, I was sympathetic towards those that did. I was certainly not embracing the patriotic mood, but again, I wasn't this, and I wasn't that, I was just what I was, which was a little bit different than everybody else and everything else.

Sally

Sometimes I'm comfortable with my American identity, and sometimes not. Last summer I went to a Blue Angels air show at the local Navy base, and I went ironically with three other English people, and my husband. There was all this patriotism around me, which is not a bad thing, but I just felt it must look really odd to these English people, this sort of rah, rah America, do or die, right or wrong kind of feeling these other people had. Granted most of the people who were there were in the military, or related to someone in the military, so there was a lot of "hard core" patriotism from these military families -- more so than anywhere else. I felt uncomfortable. I thought, America is not a perfect country and there are other countries in the world that have a lot to offer. And not everybody in every other country is dying to be American. I think a lot of Americans have a hard time accepting that anyone would want to be anything else. It was sort of embarrassing. I'm an American and I'm proud to be an American, but there are wonderful places all around the world and people have the right to be proud of that too. We have a lot of good things going for us, but we have a lot of bad things too.

CHAPTER FOUR

WHY DO I FEEL SO MIGRATORY?

Introduction

Childhood mobility of any kind seems to leave a legacy of restlessness in the adult. A kind of constant wanting to be somewhere else, but with no clear definition of where that place might be. It was interesting that almost in the same breath as the voices explained how they resisted deep commitment to a place, they said how that also enabled them to pick up and leave any time they wanted to.

It is not only the internal time clock that many of them find themselves listening to, but also the sense of freedom they may have learned as children when they knew they would eventually walk out of their history in any one place. Although painful to leave when you don't want to, there is also a sense of exhilaration in beginning again, of leaving old problems behind and unfinished business to another day. There is always the thought that in the next place they'll do better, be better, try out being someone else. No one knows you, so it is a chance to start over, reinvent yourself, create new friendships and new goals.

All of the voices have current passports, all of them feel they would be at home anywhere in the world, all of them keep up a pretext, implied or real, that they could move tomorrow if they had to. Most of them already have, in all kinds of ways, through the years. The fact that many of them have lived in the same house, the same city, the same area for years doesn't seem to change this perception. Some are restless in their careers, some move into new housing with regularity, some long for more overseas trips and have a vague notion that one day, sometime in the future, they will move overseas again if only for a little while.

While their generation is a particularly mobile one by nature, the voices seem to be particularly attuned to its calling. Conditioned by many childhood moves they have the attitude "home is where my hat is." They also seem to fully understand that when they choose to put their hat on and walk away, they better take their memories away with them because they can never return to the same place, in the same way, again. Their childhoods have been set in a series of places which disappear in meaningfulness to them the moment they leave. Their world overseas is often made up of international schools and groups of expatriate friends, that by definition, are not deeply integrated into the local culture around them. These real-life Brigadoons last only as long as a person is able to visit and to participate in its charms.

THE VOICES

Nomads in the Making

<u>Andrea</u>

We own our home. I remember when I was in high school I could never imagine owning my own home. I always thought I would just live in a tent. I just had this image. I had a friend and we were similar in that; it was just very hard to imagine all that responsibility. You would actually have to work to have to pay for this house. Just to be stuck like that. In my tent, I would work a little bit and have enough to do things, and I could do what I wanted for a while and I could just move when I wanted. And I did that for a while after I got out of high school. I did a little bit of traveling around. I think I was restless. I could just leave if I got tired of something. I remember thinking that when we went to new places I would always think "OK, now this is a whole new start. I can be whoever I want to be, nobody knows me at all." It was like a total blank. But somehow, it never worked out that way. You still couldn't reinvent yourself in each place. Habit, personality were there -- you couldn't just change yourself totally. We've lived in our house now since my son David was two, so that is four years. I don't envision change in the near future. Someday we might.

I have a current passport. I haven't really gone back to the places I've lived as a child.... I think I always knew that when you left, it would never be the same. The same people would never be there. It would just be totally different, so you couldn't really go back.

<u>Sally</u>

I have often said that my childhood was a great experience and I would do it all again. I don't have any regrets -- I don't have firm roots in any particular place, but I had such good experiences and fond memories and wonderful friends all over the country and the world, that I wouldn't trade that for anything. I would do it again. But I don't know if I will, with my own kids or whatever, but I think it was a very good experience. There were ups and downs, but there would have been ups and downs anywhere. At least I am not afraid to move somewhere. I know that I can handle moves and adjustments. If my husband's career is one that takes us places, I know that I can handle that. I won't be the kind of person who puts her foot down and says, "No I won't leave." Because I will; I've done that my whole life. It would probably feel weird to me to live somewhere for ten years.

Why Do I Feel So Restless, If I Am So Settled?

Sally

I think on the negative side, I have a tendency not to feel very settled where I am. I always seem to have this somewhat latent desire to be somewhere else, or to think about where I am going to be. I have yet to find a place where I can say, "This is where I want to be, I want to live here forever." I just don't feel that way. And I haven't. After I graduated from college I came back to Rochester Hills to live with my parents and from the minute I moved in I wanted to leave. Not because of my parents but just because this was not the place I wanted to be. And then I moved to Boston and was in Boston for only about six months because my college sweetheart came and swept me off my feet, and he lived in San Diego. When I was in Detroit I wanted to be in Boston and once I got to Boston I wanted to be in San Diego, and now that I am in San Diego I miss my friends and my Mom back in Michigan.... That sort of transient growing up experience maybe has affected (me) ... maybe there is an unwillingness or inability to feel settled as an adult.

I see my future more in terms of change than stability at this point. My husband and I have sort of envisioned where we want to live in the future, so that's more in terms of change.... I really want to show him the world from my perspective. I want to take him to England and show him where I grew up and share some of my experiences with him there. I really want to take him to Mexico. His impression of Mexico is not a good one. We live on the border near Tijuana, which is probably one of the worst representative cities that there is. He has the feeling that everyone in Mexico wants to come to the States, because everything in Mexico is so horrible and crappy and dirty and disgusting and poor. He really has a hard time believing that there are people in Mexico who love Mexico and who are proud of Mexico and want to stay in Mexico. It's not without its problems, but I think it's a wonderful place.

He is not against the idea of living overseas someday for a year or so. I don't know if this is something which will actually happen. He is not against the idea, but he's not pursuing it either. That doesn't really matter to me -- I seem to be fairly content with the way things are right now. I wouldn't be disappointed if I never lived overseas again, but if the opportunity were presented to me, I'd probably be thrilled.

Rob

I feel in constant transition. I am stable, but I still feel like I'm always living out of a suitcase. There is a feeling that events are going to take place that I have no control over. That things will come to me; I don't have to go to them. Things will happen.

Peter

Recently both my wife and I have been feeling restless. Our involvement in the church here is important, but it's not crucial to either the church or to us.... We are kind of on the periphery. Our

ministry of shelter here is not what it was before, for whatever reasons
-- people haven't called, haven't needed it. We do fan that, but it is
not our driving force. ... We've been here all these years in large part
because we haven't known where else we should go. But not because
we have a real strong commitment to this place. We're wondering if
maybe in the next year, or couple of years, we may be moving out to
a different place. There are things here -- there are the people, and we
love this house, there's the kids' school.

I don't feel marginal now. I feel integrated -- but I do feel a
restlessness.... I never expected I'd be living here this long. A big part
of being able to be here is this house. When we first saw this house
one of my first reactions was to say, "I could settle down here."

Julia

I like change.... I've been happy though to be settled
domestically. I moved here, we've stayed here. We've lived in this
house for twelve years, I've had my job for seven years. There has
been a lot of stability. I get very restless if I don't move around, go
places, but I can do that by going to an art gallery, going to
Washington or New York, it doesn't even have to be a good place to
go, it is just the physical movement that is important. I'm happy about
all this as long as the basics in my life remain stable. That's satisfied
my need for change without going overseas to live.

Barbara

I still do feel restless. I only stay in jobs about two years -- I
get really bored with jobs.

Craig

I always keep a current passport. The last time I was overseas
was 1978, but it's very important that I have an active passport. I

want to be able to get out of here whenever I want! I have not been back to the countries where I grew up. The only place I would really like to go back to probably is Bolivia -- maybe Brazil, but it was in Bolivia that I had the best time. I was there about two and a half years. I just liked it the best of all the places we lived. But I don't really want to go back in one respect, because it's going to be different (now). How could it be the same as when I was there in 1965? I'm sure things will be very different. People that I knew will not be there; I want to remember it the way I knew it and not be disappointed.

Coming to Terms with Stability

<u>Craig</u>

In terms of my future, right now I have no desire to move. Eventually I will, but I'm tired of moving, I'm tired of hassles that are connected with moving, I'm tired of making new friends. Right now I just want to stay put. I feel more comfortable in the Washington area than anywhere else because I know there are other people just like me here. I can finally say, "This is it." That's a big difference from ten years ago when I was always saying "Where am I going from here?" I was jumping from one thing to the other. I'm in a period now where it's time just to leave all that behind.

<u>Christine</u>

... I miss traveling. Even after -- even three or four years -- after Korea I was just ... I just had the bug. I just wanted to go and fly, I missed being on airplanes, and going to different countries. And then, now -- I'm very content to stay here. I don't have that itchy feeling to get away. I always want to travel. But I've always sort of wanted to sink down somewhere, just to have a home. Now I have one!

Michael

I also, up to that point, always felt -- one of the ways I rationalized joining the Foreign Service -- that given my background I had this built-in time clock. Every two, three, four years you get restless, and it's time to move again because that's what I'd been used to doing my whole life. I think that was true and it worked fine up to a point. Then I found, after five years or so in the Foreign Service, I began to rethink it and had thoughts about moving every three or four years. At this point I was in my 30s, I was faced with other kinds of decisions -- my marriage, having kids -- and I thought all this moving could really be disruptive. So, at this point, I did an about face and decided I really didn't want to keep on moving around. It took me a long time to really rationalize in my mind that that's what it was because I still enjoy traveling. I still, somewhere in my mind, think someday in my career I'll be back into something where I'll live overseas at least one more time in my life. I never can quite put the notion away totally. But I remember when I was due to go overseas again -- after five years in Washington -- I wasn't ready to go. Finally the Foreign Service said "If you want to be in the Foreign Service, being overseas is what it's all about, come on." When I thought about it and had to make up my mind, I said, "They're right," and I resigned. Part of that was because ... I gradually realized I'd switched to wanting some sort of stability -- to put my roots down here and yet still stay in some sort of international field.

Andy

Our game plan was, within a couple of years, to go back overseas and sort of recreate that expatriate life. But I found ... that ... I mean I'm glad we didn't do that. As the years went by we sort of devised certain ways to avoid doing that. It is a very provincial life in some ways, living in Nairobi or La Paz, where my wife works and travels to quite often now. It's a small number of people you work with and get to know, everyone is basically working for the same organization. If we did it now, we would regard it as a nice interlude, adventure; something I could do in between biographies.

We sort of opted for a lifestyle that we needed to make some sacrifices for. I could still.... While I have reservations about the whole expatriate thing -- I wouldn't want to do it all over again -- I do like being settled now. I think I would like some time in the next ten years to spend two years someplace knowing that I could come back. If I can get my next book done in two or three years, maybe that would be a good time to take off. I might be ready then to seep into another culture and do a good travel book.

When I was in my 20s I suddenly got very involved in doing journalism and I realized that if I went overseas, which I could have done in a long-term assignment of two or three years someplace, I wouldn't be allowed as a journalist to write freely without censoring myself or having to just write travel stories. If I wrote anything serious I'd get myself expelled. There are very few countries where that wouldn't be the case. As a journalist, I'm in a mode of observing -- watching and writing. The best stories are here, and the best sources, the best libraries, the best archives. If I'd ended up freelancing overseas I would have ended up doing interesting work, but it would have been threads. Three years here and three years there. While I grew up with that and found it quite natural and OK, I'm actually tired of traveling. I don't travel a lot now, though I wanted to travel a lot in my 20s. Every year I went overseas on some trip for stories. One year I went to London for three months and exchanged jobs with the foreign editor of The New Statesman. He took my job at The Nation. But now, I'm actually tired of travel. I want time to seep into a subject in depth. The hassles -- suitcases and airports and being so transient -- I find uncomfortable.

And Where We Go, Nobody Knows

<u>Gail</u>

One of the things I've learned about myself is that when I lived in New York City for eight years I thought, "Oh, my God, I've been in one place for eight years -- I can't believe this!" Then I realized I'd lived in four different apartments. That's when I began to realize I'm programmed for change. Also, that I felt comfortable wherever I went and that I didn't feel a real need for community. When I go on a trip somewhere it doesn't matter where it is or what culture it's in, I just feel comfortable there. I feel like I could move to any state and feel comfortable, although some places obviously would have more interest. Or just about any country would be all right. Obviously that's a direct result of my childhood. I see it as an advantage. I don't feel the loss of community.... I have a current passport. I'm always willing to go overseas if anybody offers me the slightest opportunity -- I don't care where it is. My attitude is that it's a vacation if I'm away from where I'm living. I love going to some other state because to me it's another culture.

<u>Julia</u>

Now we go overseas about once a year, or certainly every other year, usually to Europe. I feel incredibly comfortable, really buoyed up, by traveling around.... I have a conviction that I will always be comfortable out of my surroundings, or not feeling strange. I hear less mobile friends say that they worry about that.

<u>Sally</u>

I think I could feel comfortable anywhere in the world. I think there are places I would rather not be, but I think I could probably go anywhere. I have a current passport. I don't use it often -- I last went to England three years ago. But we have plans to go to England next year.

<u>Christine</u>

I feel I could adapt anywhere. I wouldn't like it, but I could. My husband and I were talking about just picking up, because we like France so much, and just moving there. The idea really appeals to me, but I just don't think I can do it. It's something we think about, but I'm not that free.... Maybe we'll retire or something, over there. Actually that's kind of funny, because we were talking about having children over there, growing up over there. I definitely wanted them to understand that kind of life, but I also wanted them to know their roots here.

CHAPTER FIVE

HERE ARE MY ROOTS

Introduction

Children who move around a lot soon learn to be a quick study in order to survive. Socially they learn to make the first moves, quickly assess the movers and shakers, observe the group norms, and make friends. During the time internationally mobile children are overseas, they usually enter a kind of socially exclusive bubble where most of the other children they meet, usually in a school where they share a common language, also move frequently from culture to culture. They all realize their existence within a particular bubble is only temporary and that they, or their friends, will move on in time. Eventually, when these children enter local schools and institutions in their countries of origin, the bubble bursts. The entire social structure resulting from their mobility collapses. Sometime -- for the first time -- they meet peers who haven't moved, haven't had to make new friends, haven't learned how to adapt. As we've seen already, when internationally mobile children come up against this situation, they tend to withdraw, retreat, marginalize. Not only are they confused about their status in this new situation, but also by their seeming inability to adapt quickly to it.

This is usually the point in time when they are described by their peers as seeming aloof and lacking in depth. Internationally mobile children now can begin to appreciate and better understand what was going on inside the bubble. Besides feeling the loss of particular friends, there is also the loss of the unique structure that nurtured those friendships. Outside that bubble they sometimes distrust their ability to make and keep good friends. That's not to say they are socially inept -- for in general they are very socially skilled at making surface acquaintances and friends. It's just that as they get older they begin to question whether they want to keep making emotional commitments to people who keep slipping away from them.

So how does this all tie in with roots? After all, internationally mobile children are rather rootless. They don't seem to bond to land or place and, except for their families, everyone else they know seems to be on a moving sidewalk flowing in the opposite direction. As adults they say they live on the surface within their communities, that they might expect to move away some day. What ties do they feel are important enough to retain as they enter mid-life?

The answer is people -- friends, and often old friends. Although they soon learn they can't bond and hold tight to everyone they meet and like, they often do hold on to some of those old friendships from their past. For it is those old friendships that validate their childhood, reaffirm those places for them and tell them something about who they were at that time. People are real -- better than pictures, better than memories. Even if they only connect with these people once a year, or see them very occasionally at school reunions, or write or call them infrequently, these connections are the bedrock of their past. While a taproot won't penetrate bedrock, equal multiple roots can spread over great distances seeking footholds to anchor the life it protects. Some come to sense this very early in their changing lives, others come to it later in life when they find they have need of more roots.

THE VOICES

People Not Place

<u>Sally</u>

I have good memories both from England and from Mexico, and I've maintained a lot of friendships with my English friends, who are all still there. I have made a few trips back to England since I left in 1975. I'd also like to go back to Mexico, although it is so different now because most of my friends are no longer there.

I felt more at home in Mexico than I did (when I went to college) in Ann Arbor. I knew I would only be temporarily living in Ann Arbor and I didn't try to put any roots down. It felt like (it was) a transient experience. I didn't feel at home there.... When I graduated from college and I didn't know what I wanted to do with myself, I moved back in with my parents -- into the small condominium. They were very gracious and let me move back in until I got my act together. I didn't know what I wanted to do, I didn't know where I wanted to go, I didn't have any friends there -- yet I couldn't go where my friends were because they were all over the place. I was really drawn to go somewhere where I knew people.... I made a somewhat feeble attempt to go to Dallas because I had some friends there and I thought I would be able to share an apartment with one of my friends. But that never worked out and I'm glad now.... But it didn't feel like my home -- my home was back in Mexico and it wasn't even my home then because all the people that made it home where gone. It was a rough time.

<u>Craig</u>

... Leaving friends had created a tremendous amount of insecurity on my part. It was very difficult to make lasting friendships because I knew that at some point in time I would have to leave and

I didn't want to be hurt. I think that has remained with me even to this day. After I left a post I got this feeling of remorse over leaving good friends. It just consumed me. I made very, very good friends overseas. For the most part, overseas kids are a very close-knit group, much more so than in this country where I think relationships tend to be cultivated over a longer period of time. Overseas you develop very strong relationships with people.

Leaving friends involuntarily -- and I think that's the key -- is very difficult. Throughout life we make conscious decisions to end relationships, friendships. We make those decisions on our own. It's a voluntary decision. The child of a foreign service officer doesn't have that liberty. Those decisions are forced upon him. I wasn't ready to break relationships with these people. But I didn't have a choice. That is very difficult.

... Now I define roots through connections and associations, shared experiences, shared backgrounds -- with people and places. Now that is finally beginning to gain on me. I am much more at ease with myself and my surroundings than I was. It's important that I know where old friends are. Even though I might not make a conscious effort to contact them, it's very important they know that I know they are there. Don't ask me why this is so. But it is important to me that I know that if I need to get in touch with them, that person is there -- at least there is a lifeline. Now they probably think I am terrible because I don't call or get in touch -- I don't necessarily need to see them or talk to them, but it's important that I know where people are. I know where so few of them are, I think that's what makes it a problem. I wish I knew where a lot more people are. I'm not close to my sister, and I'm not really close to my parents. My sister lives in Florida -- she's married and has kids. My parents are down in Naples, Florida. I call my sister on her birthday and when something is wrong with my parents, and that's about it. What I am talking about is my own network, the one I've made.

Michael

I don't belong to lots of organizations here in Washington --
civic leagues and things like that. But I do have a stake here in terms
of the friends I've developed in the Washington area. That's
something too that's had a big effect on me from my upbringing in the
Foreign Service since I'd never been good at keeping in touch with
people. I'd go overseas, be there for a few years, develop some close
friendships, and then move on somewhere else. I think that I found --
and also my friends in the Foreign Service found -- that you're
changing environments so constantly it's hard to keep track of where
people are and it's an age, at least here in the States, where we are so
used to picking up the phone to be in touch with someone instead of
writing. You lead such busy and hectic lives living in the city. I've
never been good at correspondence, writing letters. Actually I always
found it easier overseas, because I had more time to do that. Here I
work ten or eleven hours and when I go home from work, I'm
exhausted. On the weekends there's always distractions. So I found
it hard keeping in touch with people. Throughout my childhood all
my friendships were fairly transient but once I was in the Washington
area, when I came back from Haiti in 1983, I guess that was a real
changing point for me. The friendships that I've had here have been
the longest term friendships I've had at any time of my life. And I've
gotten to an age where they mean more to me. Part of that was
influenced by the fact that when I got back from Haiti I went through
a divorce, and it was a lesson in the value of having close friends. I
put a lot of value on the friendships I have in the Washington area,
and those made me want to have a stake in one place.

Fighting to Keep the Ties Tight

<u>Barbara</u>

Thankfully I'm not restless about relationships. I am extremely loyal as a friend -- if you've befriended me, you're a friend for life.

I tried keeping up friends all through my childhood and high school years, unfortunately they've been the ones -- they got married, or they moved or something happened that they didn't keep up. Even in college I was in touch with friends from when I was ten years old in Cyprus, and six years old in Denver, but they got married, or moved on in life, and that's been really hard for me. There are some people I really felt close to and I wish they'd kept up. I don't feel rejected, I just feel -- once my parents die, my father's already died, once my mother dies -- they are the only contacts to the past I had and to the kind of person I was.

My closest friends now are from college. Every time I come back to the States now I write all these people that I'd gotten out of touch with for one reason or another. I just got a letter from a friend I met when I was 18 and went to college. He's now married, and I hadn't been in touch with him for five years. It's so good to be back in contact with him. He remembers me from when I was 18 and in a way that is refreshing because you can stand back and say, "Well, I don't do that any more." or "Oh yes, isn't that wonderful that you remember that I did that." You can't remember everything and vice versa.

Sarah

I still retain some of my friendships from high school in Tangier and from college. My brother thinks I'm tenacious about my relationships and how I keep up. I'm coordinator here for the Returned Peace Corps Volunteer network for Togo.

Sally

I do work to keep friendships up. I am on vacation right now and I've just seen a couple of different friends here that I hadn't seen for a long time. The last time I was here I did that too. I try to write letters, but I often fall short of my own goals. But I don't like to see friendships sort of slide away. I think I should be able to maintain them through the years and I think I do a pretty good job -- even when I don't have anything in common with them anymore, we'll still be friends.

I don't like to lose friendships, but I can see how everyday life sort of gets in the way of things like that.... Some friendships are easy to let go and others are not. Sometimes it is disappointing when I lose track of someone.

Andrea

In the beginning I did try to correspond with my friends from India. One summer after we came back from India one girlfriend came to Nantucket for a little while and we really had fun. They were there a week and we were there a month. Then everybody scattered again. I only heard about her through my mom. We didn't actually write each other again until we became adults. She was in northern Virginia for a while when I was there in school at Montgomery College and I saw her once or maybe twice.

Rob

... I make friends easily, but in terms of close friends, maybe two or three. And they've been my friends for 20 - 22 years -- as long as my wife and I have been married. And I have my buddy Andy in Virginia Beach. I met him at Camp Mohawk in Salisbury, England. The American Youth Association camp was run by Americans on the Salisbury Plain, about 30 miles away from Stonehenge. The camp was on the grounds of an old abbey. The abbey had been rebuilt and there were still monks there. I remember the monastery, the vineyards. We went in the summer of 1964 -- we were both assigned to the Hopi Indian tribe! We hit it off together. We watched some of the monks ride up on their bikes to go to work in the field. We played a little hooky and took their bikes and rode down into the town -- just to see what was going on. We bought some cigarettes, and I smoked my first cigarette -- I got sick as a dog. I couldn't ride the bicycle, I had to walk it all the way back up the hill to exactly where we found them. No one ever said a word.

Christine

It's difficult for me to find friends. I guess, people that I hang out with, maybe at work ... it's always been through work or school that I've met people. I never really have full, solid friendships. There is always a little distance in there. And I've never really kept in touch with a lot of friends -- close friends. At the time we were close, and then I've left, or whatever, and I've never gotten back in touch with them since. There is one exception in that I've kept in touch with three women I went to school with in Pakistan. We were a gang of five. We were known as the "Odd Squad." They were some of the funniest people. Two of them I just tried to relocate recently, after many years. One was in Maine and now she's in Norfolk, Virginia. The other one -- I remembered her mother lived in McLean, Virginia, and then I remembered they moved away. They were with AID and her father was killed at the American Embassy in Beirut during the bombing. My friend's mother was badly injured herself. I never got back in touch with my friend after that to express my condolences. I lost touch with her, but just the other week -- I've been feeling these ties to these people -- I tried to contact them again. I called my friend's mother, she was back in town, and she told me that my friend is now in Arizona. But those are the only ones I really feel close to. I'm sure we're totally different now and we probably don't have anything in common. But of course, we do have one thing in common.... It will be interesting to see both of them again.

Gail

I have a few very strong friends. It's interesting, because my pattern is to have a few really close friends and lots of happy nodding acquaintances. It takes me a long time to make friends -- a long time. I'm open and I'm warm and in my profession I have had to learn how to be that way, even though I'm naturally sort of a shy person.... So I'm able to make superficial friends and have fun with people, but it takes me a long time to really open up to other people. I think that's a function of losing friends over and over again. I need to be able to trust they'll be around. If they've been around after three or four years maybe I can start opening up to them -- it looks as though they are not moving ... maybe.

... ironically, in the past few years, the person I most consistently do social things with is my sister. We had this big hiatus when we weren't anywhere near each other. We'd shared a room for years; you know, her bed would be under the light switch but it would be my turn to turn off the light that night and I'd have to get out of bed and walk across the room to turn off the light and then try to go back to sleep. "Can't you just reach your arm up?" "No, it's your turn!" It was that kind of a relationship.

... my best friend now is someone I went to high school with in India. And it's funny because we were friends in India, but we weren't really close friends. You never know afterwards who's going to end up sticking with you and who isn't; sometimes it's the most improbable people. We had been corresponding and then I ended up coming back to this country after Peace Corps and we started hanging out together on vacations and found what a connection there was between us for all sorts of reasons. Part of it was that we felt so comfortable with each other because of our backgrounds. That has persisted in being my most significant friendship. And she lives in Kentucky, so that makes it a bit hard.

One of the people at my school happened to be my best friend when I was in fifth grade in Ghana. Her son goes to my school now. It's so weird. I use her as an example; I say ... at back- to-school night, "look around you at all the people sitting next to you. Your children will run into their children 30 years from now in some obscure country in the middle of Eastern Europe or somewhere." ... We don't see each other very often, but there's a real connection. That is the gut connection I have with this school here too. That's why I feel so comfortable here. I have an emotional kind of attachment and a recognition that's really important too.

Craig

I can identify certain periods in my life. When I hear a song I can identify the song, I know exactly when that song came out -- Bolivia periods, Brazil periods. My memory is very compartmentalized. It was very difficult when I came back to Philadelphia during home leave and the kids didn't recognize me because they had moved on to other events and I hadn't. I had left them. They vaguely remembered me, and I remembered them very well. I'd held on to them all my life. To this day I continually think about people that I knew and wonder where they are. I am trying to get a Bolivia reunion going through Overseas Brats. But it seems it is going to be next to impossible. I don't know how to do it, really. The only thing I can think of is to put a classified ad in the Overseas Brats newsletter. The problem really is with the women because they change their names when they marry.

I've been trying to find this old girl friend of mine from Brazil, just to tell her she was important to me growing up. Those bonds are so important. But I can't find her.

When I was a freshman in college there was a reunion of some of the people from Bolivia, and I was really excited about that. That was the last time I saw anyone I knew overseas with one or two exceptions. There was one additional time in Tennessee -- I drove down with a girl I was dating at the time and there were friends from Morocco and Bolivia who were there. That was the last contact I think I've had with anyone from my childhood overseas. That was 1970, maybe. There is one exception -- that's true. I stumbled upon an old classmate from Morocco in college, at a Vietnam war demonstration. I got bopped over the head by a cop. I bumped into him then. I recognized him. Even now someone that I knew in sixth grade, if I saw them today, I could probably recognize them. I'm at a point now where I'm starting to forget names. For the longest time I forced myself to remember names, but I'm starting now to forget people's names that I knew. But if I saw them, I'd recognize them. The whole experience left such an indelible imprint.

What every kid who grows up like I did knows is that "I was there, I did live there." Now it is difficult to reconnect with the people that know I was there -- because they were there too. That's why the reunions are so important to me, so it won't seem all a dream and evaporate without any connection. It helps convince me in my own mind that I was there! It's a connection with the reality.

Julia

Last year I went to a reunion of the New Delhi class of 1965-66.... An amazing number of us gravitated to the East Coast from various backgrounds, so a lot of us were in the general area.There were only 21 in my class, I believe, but most came to the reunion. One guy who got to Delhi on sort of a fluke, his father was some sort of contract technician, felt his years in Delhi had been the highlight of his life. He became dedicated to finding the others he went to school with. About ten years ago, he found us all....   I'd changed my name, my place of residence. After he found all of us, a group of people began to put together a network and a few really kept it together and organized. (We) had a big reunion in Lake Tahoe and for our 25th reunion we are planning to go back to India. The incredible thing is that everybody wanted to be there, even though we'd mostly been out of touch for many years.

One guy who came was arrested in Thailand for selling heroin shortly after we graduated and had been in jail until just last year. All that time -- it was awful. We all knew he was there. Our mothers networked with us to channel him presents and notes for 20 plus years. And he came to this party.

Those years in Delhi were among the happiest times of my life. My husband was absolutely amazed, he was astonished, by the character and caliber of the people there at the reunion -- and by their attachment to each other. This group of kids came from a lot of different economic backgrounds. None of that seemed to matter and that's not as true here. There were different nationalities. None of that made much difference. Yet we were very different. Some ... did not have the same aspirations, and were probably not going on to college. But they were still part of the group because we were a group. There were no cliques. We were having a wonderful time. India was such a wonderful place to be.... We only had to walk down the street and there were the Lodi tombs. I think there was so much to take up our energies and imaginations. That made it very easy for us to be friends.

Rob

Our high school in London has reunions. As a matter of fact we had the first two reunions at our house for about four or five classes. About 50, 60 people showed up. That wasn't as large as the one I went to in Houston, Texas.   All the teachers showed up from

Central High School. There must have been four to five hundred people starting from the class of 1954 right through to `86.  There were five of us from the class of `68. There are a lot of alums in Texas because a lot of them were in the Air Force, and they'd been meeting there for years. It was huge and took up two hotels. They had the ambassador and consul general from Britain come and make speeches. I got to see some teachers. I remember going up to my English teacher and saying hello, introducing myself. "Oh, you're the troublemaker." Apparently I had a reputation.

CHAPTER SIX

SERIOUS COMMITMENTS:
MARRIAGE AND CAREER

Introduction

If in mid-life the voices are still a bit restless, they don't seem restless about their marriage partners and their career choices. On the contrary, in those areas they seem to be relatively settled. Part of their stability may be attributed to the fact that their families of origin were uniquely strong and stable; not one of them has divorced parents. The conventional wisdom concerning couples overseas was that it quickly breaks a bad marriage and cements a good one.

What is interesting is that most of the partners the voices chose share to some degree their own marginality, and in some cases even their mobile childhood. Two spouses are children of American military families. Five are married to religious minorities and/or first-generation immigrants to the United States. Only two married spouses from mainstream, rooted families with lots of history and attachment to a place -- both of those spouses by coincidence were from Long Island. One of those marriages ended in divorce.

As to choice of career, the voices expressed a need for a lot of autonomy in their careers. They seem more competent than outwardly competitive in their careers. Instead, they prefer to write their own job descriptions, even if it means less income. Predominately they are in or aspire to service occupations. For instance, two make their living by watching and interpreting -- one as a military investigator and one as a writer of biographies on national political figures. Only one is working for a "Fortune 500" company.

Some of the voices explain that there seems to be a link between seeing so much poverty and suffering as children and wanting to help people in their careers.

One commitment they seem to lose over the course of their childhood is a commitment to an organized faith or religion. While some of them had religious instruction or attended churches overseas, all but one has moved away from the religious origins they had as children. This may be partly just lack of opportunity as they were growing up, but it may also be in part because they were exposed to so many other religious faiths and beliefs in the various cultures where they lived.

THE VOICES

Of Lovers and Spouses

<u>Andy</u>

I can remember feeling a great deal of resentment and anger that I couldn't engage people on the Palestinian issue. By the time I met my wife, I was already beginning to drift away from the issue, even though it was to be my senior thesis at Carleton. My experience in Beirut had sort of underscored for me how difficult, how intractable, it was. Also I was realizing, as I tried to raise the subject back here in America, what a no-win hard nut it was; you couldn't get people to engage on it. I was beginning to decide ... this was not an issue I wanted to devote my life to. It would be a matter of facing defeat after defeat. In a way, meeting her, allowed me to engage on it at a personal level.... We had a lot in common as a result of her being Jewish.... It was important to me that I could be able to explain the issue to someone like her. She, as a Jew in America, was like a foreigner; she can feel the same sort of distance that I felt in being an expatriate. (And) not only is she Jewish, but her parents are holocaust survivors. Her father spent most of the war in a camp in Italy, although he was from Vienna. He escaped from Austria in `39 and ended up being arrested by the Italians and spending three years in a camp in Southern Italy. Her mother's mother had died before the war, but her mother and her mother's father had escaped from ... Austria, and moved to Yugoslavia where they had relatives. He was picked up by the Nazis and put into a Yugoslavian concentration camp where he died a year later.

... Obviously I knew Norah was Jewish, and I told myself it didn't matter. Now that I look back, I realize it mattered a lot.

Now, with Norah in the same (kind of international) business, in effect ... for almost 20 years, we've been separated every year for at least three months and often some years it was six months all together -- six weeks here, a month there, a couple of weeks there. Obviously, one reason I've been able to deal with that -- put up with that -- was that I had a lot of practice saying goodbye to people, and then picking up again. I always think she'll come back, but just as in recent years I have gotten tired of traveling, I sort of regard the time we're not together as wasted time. I put up with it.

Julia

I thought my husband was pretty representative of his American culture when I first met him, but.... He grew up in Pittsfield, Massachusetts, and his parents were both Jewish immigrants who had come to this country from Russia, many in their families were killed in the holocaust. Consequently he grew up with a lot of anxiety in the home, underneath, even though his parents seemed to have done a really good job of raising him to feel secure and safe and protected. His parents really couldn't talk about what had happened in Europe. Pittsfield was a place with a very small Jewish community, there was some underlying discrimination that they always knew was there. So a lot of his stories are about establishing himself. He was a great big strapping kid and he had to fight for who he was. Like me, he's had to work at it -- deciding who I was and how to explain to other people how I got that way. So even though in many superficial ways we are very different -- age difference, cultural backgrounds -- actually we have a lot in common....

There were three couples at the reunion of my New Delhi high school class -- six people -- who got married just after our senior year, and are still married and give every indication of being very happy. Given the vast changes in our lives, not to mention in America, it's not what you would expect. My impression was too that this group had much more stable marriages in general than any other group I know. Of course, there had been some divorces, some changes. But maybe they came from a position of having to be more flexible, more adaptable. That's a key to making it work. And the ability to get your identity from yourself -- knowing you have to do it by yourself. I think foreign service kids are less likely, at least those that I know, to make the mistake of getting their identity from someone else. That can be a real obstacle in some relationships.

<u>Michael</u>

I had, until recently, always gone out with Protestant women. We used to joke in the family. My sister (will marry) someone just like my father, and I'll marry someone just like my mother. Then three years ago I met someone new and we got married, and she's Jewish. So that's why I've been more conscious of it recently.... My mother is very involved with family history. She's researched the whole family, which has been easy to do because her family goes back a long way and it's documented. My father's father was a Russian immigrant. There is nothing to trace after that. In that sense I've always been aware of the contrast but I never thought about it as truly cross-cultural. Maybe because my mother has always had more influence on us. She would talk about her family and her family's history, she would take us to church. My father never talked about his family. We had no sense of any family history there, we didn't even know where in Russia my grandfather had come from. Only as adults have we been more interested and tried to ask my father. My father was always more concerned about his future and didn't want to think too much about his past. My mother is just the opposite. If my father had talked a lot more about his father's heritage or his religion, then we might have been more aware of it and the contrast.

I met my first wife while I was (working for) the Peace Corps. Then when we went on our first tour with the Foreign Service to Haiti, she worked for the AID mission there. She had a stable childhood. She joined the Peace Corps thinking she'd been in the same place all her life and now wanted something different. Her father was a journalist and had been a foreign correspondent for ABC, and, although she hadn't traveled, she heard all his tales when he'd been traveling. Her father was a big influence on her and she thought it important to go out and see the world.... But that marriage ended in divorce. I got remarried to someone not in international work.

My present wife is from Atlanta. She spent her entire life there. We talk about this a lot -- she still has friends going back to when she was in first grade, five years old. She is still in touch with a dozen people that she went all the way through school with. They are still very close. Just out of college she spent a year in Brazil, and then traveled a fair amount. She has a more worldly exposure and some of the same interests that I do.

Rob

I got married in June 1971 to Jane, whose father was a colonel in the Marine Corps. We met in high school, we met in London. There wasn't a lot of pressure on us to get married, but we both felt we'd been around the world, we'd seen everything; if we don't get married ... it was couched in terms of going off to war. We just wanted to seize the moment. We approached Jane's parents with the idea of getting married and they said wait until Jane's father gets back from Vietnam. So we waited from 1970 to 1971. My mother also died two weeks before we were to get married. Then Jane and I were on our own to live here in the United States. She had gone from base to base as a child, went through the same sort of thing as I had in her life -- two years here, two years there. She was ready to settle down. For the first ten years of our marriage all we did was travel -- all the money we earned we spent traveling. We were out in Wyoming, Utah, Oregon, California, Laguna Beach, Ft. Lauderdale. We were looking for a place. That's when I first realized the size and scope of this country.... Rather than spend money to go back to Europe to revisit -- which I'd like to do one day, especially London where we still have friends -- we'd spend money and see the United States.

Barbara

I met my husband after a full day horseback riding out in Maryland, and I had just voted for Mondale and I went to a mutual friend's house, who had the only TV ... and I met him there through that friend. I was liberal and he was conservative.

He had always had world interests. His father is Austrian. His father married a lady from a small town in Illinois. He was always interested in living in Europe, and then he got into the Foreign Service and (was) sent to Haiti. He wasn't so wild about that, but we had a blast there and now he's interested in going anywhere in the world. We went to Germany after that because we wanted something staid and then the wall broke in Germany, and it was all so very exciting. After this assignment he's talking about Burma, maybe Cambodia. All the places that are still exotic and haven't been changed by Western culture.

... I also think it's really important that my husband and I have the same kind of outlook and relationship as my parents. I really believe that if you travel, your parents are your identity. They are the cohesiveness to your future and how you are going to develop. If they waver away from their marriage or the goals of their lives, then the kids will get screwed up. The other roots -- being in the same place, having the same friends all the time -- just aren't there. So you have to have the same parents all the time.

Andrea

I'm in a very settled period now. I like how my life is now. I've been married since 1984 -- almost ten years. My husband is a landed person. But his parents threw him a wrench. They moved to Brazil when he went to college -- for job related reasons.... He's not really international, except that he is in a way -- he's an immigrant. At age one and a half he immigrated with his family from England. His father is Russian. There is background stuff. He is also part Scottish. They went to Brazil because his dad didn't like the way he was being treated here in his job. His dad is a scientist, a physicist. He took a position in Brazil at the university.

Craig

But I married the person I did, someone who was a local girl -- I was looking for that. She's totally the antithesis of me, totally the opposite. But there was stability there that I'd never had. And there is a mother in there too. She mothers me and babies me. There were certain things about her that attracted me to her. The relationship has gone through some rocky times too, but it's long term -- we've managed to keep it together. I don't know what is going to happen when we see each other every day, but it's been ten years now.

My wife works in New York and commutes to Virginia on the weekends. When we were living together in this small town on Long Island, I hated it. She was from that town, knew everybody -- I hated it. I could not identify with these people at all. To me, I felt I had nothing in common with anybody there. I refused to get involved in any of the community things. I felt totally as though I was in a closet and couldn't get out. I felt so stifled. I felt I just needed to escape. It was totally different than anything I had ever experienced. The idea of people living in the same town all their lives -- I had nothing in common with these people!

During the week now she lives with her parents. They live about five minutes away from where she works. Every Friday she catches the plane to National and leaves Monday morning. Unorthodox! She is very close to her parents and her school age friends. She can't quite understand why I am just the opposite.

Although I like her parents very much, I don't have this need to see them on a regular basis. Holidays are fine for me. But she is very close to them. We're totally opposite.

Gail

There wasn't a thing international about my husband. I met him two months before I was to go off to the Peace Corps and maybe I needed some kind of an anchor or something, I'm not sure. He was just a very nice person who was paying attention to me and we had a wonderful time together. We really enjoyed each other's company. And yet he was somebody who had never been off Long Island except to go to Bard. After Bard he immediately went back to Long Island and is still there today.

He was a WASP, but what the hell is a WASP doing at Bard College? He automatically had to be different. He's obviously got a screw loose there somewhere. And yet he went back to this Waspy family on Long Island, which is just straight down-the-line Episcopalian, old family, etc. So I must have been attracted to that -- I must have sensed that was something that was different. Anybody that's at Bard is a little bit different and interesting anyway. Maybe that in combination with the stability: always from Long Island from a family that stretched way back, you know.

And yet, when I was looking for someone else, it was the exact opposite. I go back to my roots, somebody who's got all the same interests in terms of being raised overseas. It provided me with that other set of insights and connections that I hadn't had in my marriage.

I met him at my high school reunion. The Delhi reunion. I immediately made this connection. At that point I was thinking about getting ready to move from Long Island to Washington. I came down to Washington for this reunion and met this old friend -- a passing friend. Everybody's a friend when you're in high school and there are only 75 people in your class. We made this immediate "click" and I think maybe I needed another anchor to get me from Long Island down to Washington. So we carried on this relationship for a year while I was trying to decide whether to go into the Foreign Service or move to Boston; or, whether to move to Washington and move down here with him and live with him, as I did for five years in a disastrous relationship. I got out of it about two years ago.

Of Careers and Goals

Craig

I was always looking for some excitement in my life. I'm not the type who is going to be happy working in a shoe store. How do you compare that with Foreign Service life? Everything else is anti-climatic. I kicked around a lot looking....

Andy

I basically left home when I was 16 by going to boarding school. From a very young age I traveled a lot by myself. That was good. But it prepared me to deal with loneliness too, and do things on my own. But that can be good. For instance, writing a book is a very lonely experience.

Peter

In terms of where I am now and where I want to go, I hope to make a change in my secular career. What I want to do is get into consulting with regard to intercultural conflicts, management consulting -- conflict resolution, conflict management. I hope to work with companies both American and international where they are dealing with cultural problems and conflicts. Again, whether it is related to childhood cultures or just problems within the culture, I've seen, looking back at my own experiences, how I've been helpful and instrumental in situations like this. Although I've missed a lot of American cues, one of the reasons for that was I didn't think I needed to pick up on them. I assumed I knew it. But in other situations, where I know I don't know, I listen for them and I do pick up on them. This is also part of the ten-year reentry that I've been talking about. That's also taught me a lot. Even when you think you understand, you probably don't. So that's helped me too to listen. So I feel like I have skills in those areas, and that's the area I really want to put those skills to use. I'm not interested in technology, even though I'm in a technical career. Well, I am interested and I like to perfect my technical skills, but it's not my strength. My strength is in helping people work together. So that's the direction I want to go.

Julia

I grew up in an idealistic household and one which felt very strongly about public service. I was always interested in politics.

My undergraduate degree was in child development. I was interested in psychology but I became very involved in politics and ... I sort of stumbled into the career I have now. In terms of my study of psychology, I have always been -- like a lot of kids who've grown up this way -- very introspective. I don't think I wanted to learn more about myself necessarily. I think I went into child development mostly because I was interested in finding out how culture shaped a person, finding out how much of what you are is the culture you are from.

Andrea

I think in terms of my career relating to my experiences, I think I do want to help people. Physical therapy does that, people start feeling better, things happen. Usually you are causing some improvement. India was really kind of haunting in that sense. There

were so many people, and you couldn't really help them. I remember
all the beggars. You couldn't give them money, because if you did,
then there would be more and more people surrounding you.... You'd
be driving down the road and someone would be collapsed in the
middle of the road. The problem was huge.... I think in the sense that
you want to do something for people, there is a connection with what
I do now.

Gail

I have a position at (an) international school, which is just
perfect. That's the closest thing to being overseas with my daughter.
It's worked out pretty well in that respect.

I might consider going to an overseas school. Once my
daughter goes off to college, that's something I would definitely like
to consider. After being at (this) school and being back in an
environment where I'm around lots of people from different countries,
which I hadn't been in my working life previously, I realize how
comfortable I am, and how I can pass for American very easily when
I'm in an American job.

That was a whole part of me not being tapped or used before
and I realized it by the hunger I had; how I would pounce on someone
from overseas who would come to the school where I was working in
New York City. I remember when a South African family showed up
and we formed this immediate friendship. We could talk about places
we'd been in common. I just didn't have anyone to talk to about those
things. It remains buried until the opportunity comes, and then it all
springs up again. That's when you realize how much you hunger for
it.

Being in my present job is like the most fulfilling professional
environment I could imagine. It's education, which I ended up in
accidentally anyway. It's worked out really well for me and my own
particular checkered background. I don't think it could be much better
really.

Christine

You can either go one way or the other with this childhood experience. You can either focus on your experiences and put them to use or you get a lot of interests and you don't know what to do. I have a lot of interests, but I don't know where to focus....

... I want to work with children. I contacted the Foreign Service Youth Foundation and I thought I would like to help with that. I think it would be more of a catharsis for me. I would like to be with people who are like me, when I was their age. That's what I would like to do. I would also like to be a specialist or something in music education or musical therapy. Something where I feel needed. Doing something for other people, not lawyers.

Sally

In terms of my career, I like what I do and I find it rewarding, but it's not the most important thing in my life. My life is what I do outside of work and my career is what I do to support what I do outside of work. My dad was not a workaholic -- he worked regular hours and I think that sort of carried over to me. I've never been a workaholic. I can go through spurts of putting in some overtime, but as a rule I don't like it and I don't believe in it. I think I should be able to get my work done in 40 hours and then I want to go home and do whatever it is that I do. I have a fulfilling career, but it's not my life. For now I expect to work at my job indefinitely. I'm a technical writer and editor, and I've also done some training. I don't want to have to work full time when my husband and I have kids, but I'm hoping that by being an editor I can do some freelance or part-time work. I grew up with my mom at home and I would like to be able to provide that for my kids if at all possible. We'll have to see....

If I could do anything I would quit and travel! But I'm a firm believer in having to like what you are doing. I don't hate my job -- I don't always love it, but it's what I do. In terms of what you are supposed to get out of life, I think you are supposed to enjoy the ride and I'm pretty content with what I am doing right now and where I am in life. Maybe some people would fault me for not having very many goals, but my goal is to enjoy what I am doing at that moment with some thought to what I'll be doing in the future.

CHAPTER SEVEN

COSTING OUT THE PAIN

Introduction

Major mobility is never without its toll. Yet one gains immensely in perspective, in friendships, and in appreciation. All that becomes captured and stored in the memory when you move on. But the repeated lesson in loving and leaving eventually teaches you to keep your distance, to not love so much. For children growing up, expanding social horizons outside the family and searching for their own identities, this lesson is particularly cruel. While the voices could choose to keep their emotional distance as they got older, as children they desperately tried to fit in and belong.

Inevitably, at times the pain became unbearable. Feelings of anger, depression and confusion often were etched indelibly into their personal histories. These feelings are common to most mobile children -- and also to the adults who move them. The one difference is that an adult has some vestige of free will, a child has none over a geographical move. Support systems in place adjust and change with each move. If the support system is lost entirely, it takes even longer to recreate another one.

The task of starting all over again takes an enormous toll in energy and emotion. Leave-taking is often glossed over in the rush to move on. The physical work of moving, coupled with the feeling of forward momentum, often results in exhaustion and ambivalence. Anyone who has moved with any regularity or over long distances knows this is true.

There is little parents seem to do, or often can do, to protect their children from the emotional uprooting required by a geographical move. And while parents may be seen by their children as masters of anticipation, they may in fact be denying some of their own grief and frustration. Honesty and integrity about where you've been gets muddled by the tricks human nature plays in order to break away, whether it's been the best -- or the most unpleasant -- place in the world.

It sometimes came as a surprise to both parents and young adults to find how unprepared the children were to be left in their own country while their families remained or moved back overseas, or to be left on their own in a boarding school or college. Even though these culturally mobile children had been coping and adapting all their lives, they had not been left to do it entirely alone. Their very family closeness left them bereft and unprepared.

Perhaps it is just that very memory of the emotional turmoil, the enervating thought of starting all over again, that keeps the voices more or less in one place as they reach midlife, even though they say they resist staying in one place.

As the voices came to understand that they are a minority in their own country, some realize all too well that they were a privileged minority in the foreign countries where they lived as children, and that the poverty around them was very real. Sometimes this resulted in a burden of guilt that was hard to shake, even after they came home to their own country. Some were faced with outward discrimination overseas as Americans even though they didn't fully understand what it meant to be an American. One experienced what he considered to be religious discrimination.

Although as adults most of the voices have a "no pain, no gain" attitude now about their childhoods, a few are still quite resentful. Some wonder what kind of people they would be today if they hadn't had those experiences.

THE VOICES

Yeah, There Were Times I Was Really
Angry and Upset

Craig

I've never, ever heard my parents say, "Gee, it must have been hard on you, all the moving." I think I still harbor a lot of resentment. They took me from a relatively normal childhood environment and threw me into this whirlwind. It wasn't all bad, don't misunderstand me, but I think people do need to realize it does have a lasting effect. Every person reacts differently. Some will say, "This is the greatest thing that ever could have happened to me." Others say the opposite, and then there are people like me who are somewhere in the middle. It depends on the child. I had eight years of stability and then was suddenly uprooted from my grandparents, from friends, from a lifestyle, from everything. I was thrown into this unnatural situation. What I thought didn't matter, not to say that a nine year old child should necessarily make the decision whether to go or not. I think a lot of it was a certain sensitivity on my part.... My sister was more rebellious, I was more passive. I did as I was told. But inside there was a lot going on. I tried to reach out, but I never felt comfortable about it with my parents.

My parents were the type that when a two year tour was up said, "Sell as much as you can, get rid of as much as you can." Their response would be, "We'll just replace it when we get to the new post." They didn't associate possessions with feelings or attachments. But (those things) go beyond the material, they have meaning to us. We had dogs we had to leave behind. "We're not going to the expense of transporting a dog." They were very practical. That made me feel terrible. It was very difficult leaving a pet behind, but my parents thought nothing of it. It was a terrible feeling of loss. But, at that time I didn't realize it, (I) just accepted it.

It wasn't until much later, and it wasn't until I got married -- I married a local girl who had lived in the same town all her life -- that I realized how much of an effect this all had on me. For example, I'll give you an idea. This might sound pretty silly, but I had a nail clipper that for some reason I was able to hold on to from Morocco to Bolivia. I think I had this nail clipper for four years, the only thing I ever had that long. Finally I lost that nail clipper. I was devastated, not because I lost the nail clipper, which probably cost me 50 cents at the (Post Exchange), but because I had managed to hold on to this thing for so long. Everything else was -- "get rid of it." We didn't even have our own furniture overseas, the furniture was loaned to us.

My parents did distinguish between things that were indigenous to the country we were living in and things easily replaceable like record players and television sets -- things that were important to me as a kid. I remember having to sell my record player before I left Brazil because they didn't want to take it. We could get another one when we got back to the States. At that age a record player is an important object. Everything became expendable basically. Friendships were expendable, pets were expendable, possessions were expendable....

Gail

We were in Munich two and a half years. From there we went to India, in April of my tenth grade year. It was "one of those" moves. We were told about (it) three weeks ahead of time -- pack your bags you're moving to India. At least it feels as though it was three weeks. We said, "Why didn't you tell us earlier?" ... They wanted to make sure they knew something before they disrupted our lives. We knew we might move, but we didn't realize it would be so soon, I think. We had been three years in Ghana before we went to

Germany. Our very first posting was in India for five years. We weren't used to the "two year, two year" kind of thing.

I remember the only time of my life when I ever had really terrible "Delhi belly," as we used to call it in India, was the night before we left for India when we were still in Munich. Every 17 minutes I would have these terrible intestinal cramps and I was sitting in the bathroom the whole night long. Obviously, that was so clearly emotional, tied to this impending move. And to leave in the middle -- or towards the end -- of the year. I arrived just on the night of "the prom" in India, big deal -- what good does that do?

But the very interesting thing is that I went into that school in India, and I'd come from Munich, which was higher on the "cool" hierarchy than India, obviously, because I was closer to the sources of music, clothes and stuff like that. I came, apparently, looking very "cool." And at that point I really was "cool" in terms of the way I dressed and what I knew about the culture. But I immediately attached myself to an uncool group. I found out later that cool people had tried to approach me, but I had not felt like I was a cool person inside, so I had attached myself to these really nice, lovely people who are sort of the backbone of many high schools and who can end up being very good friends, but who are not the movers and shakers in the high school. It was a big high school for overseas, about 350 kids.

I immediately classified myself back to my experience of going from Ghana to Munich; again I saw myself as a totally uncool person. I suppose I thought I was going to have to repeat the experience. As it turns out, it needn't have been true at all. I eventually found the right friends for myself, but I kept being surprised.

It was a funny kind of evolution in my own mind about myself as a social being; how you define yourself based on one experience and then trying to put yourself back in that context. You lose a little momentum in terms of your self-image each time you move.

Christine

One time I came home from school and my parents asked how I would feel about moving again. "We're going to have to move and we have two choices." There was nothing I could do about it, so I said, "Well, it's OK. We're moving." It was all downhill from there. When we got to Korea I was terribly homesick. I had my guitar and I would just console myself with that. I would sit on the back steps and sing melancholy songs and just sit there and sulk. I turned really inward. That's how I expressed myself. I wrote songs, sad songs.... I expressed grief through my music. There was a lot coming out.

I was definitely relieved to leave Korea, but I remember thinking (when) I left Pakistan ... I was really happy to leave there. Not because I didn't have fun there, but because -- it's harder. I wanted to leave some memories behind....

Andrea

I know I really didn't like leaving Garmisch. That was the first time that I remember not liking to leave. But I really wasn't allowed to talk about that, or it felt like that was really being pushed aside. It was so disregarded. I didn't get any inkling how my younger siblings were feeling about the move. I was happy that this friend Karen, who I'd met in Garmisch, was supposed to be going to Moscow too. I was happy that at some point she was supposed to show up. We all packed into the car, all our possessions are away, and it was hard.

I really don't have any memories of leaving at that point. One thing about my family, and especially my father, is that they hide their feelings a lot. My mother, to a certain extent, only expresses positive feelings. So you only talk about the good. "You're going to do this, it's going to be fun." There's no talk about the past or what you're leaving, or any of that kind of stuff. That feeling dynamic -- that my parents were like that -- made these transitions much harder than they really had to be. It wasn't totally the fault of the situation.

... I don't think I ever got a chance to express grief in a proper way for the things I left behind. I think the only time I really did it was just by holing up and saying "No, I won't go to school." I think I just kind of walled it up, but I didn't really realize that I was upset. But I was upset....

My mom decided that when the school year was over ... we'd go back. That meant go to D.C. and find a place. We had to rent.... What I did -- I just said I felt sick as soon as I found out, which was two weeks before school let out. I wouldn't go to school. My mom took me for all these tests; "Did I have mono?" Here's this good student who won't go to school. They took blood and nothing was wrong with me. She told me later she had this friend of hers who was a psychologist come to the house to talk to me. The psychologist said to her, "It's OK, it's just her mind. She doesn't want to say good-bye." So my mom let me stay out of school. I do remember though going back to say good-bye. One thing that was hard was that my mom stayed right next to me and it was difficult with my boyfriend and girlfriends, it was awkward. I didn't realize that the only reason I was doing it was that I felt bad about leaving. I really thought I was sick. I felt real lethargic, headaches. I really did feel bad.

I didn't want to leave, but I knew.... I felt I probably wouldn't see these people again. It was really the end.... I had no forwarding address. You couldn't even write me in care of my father at the State Department, because he wasn't going to be there either. It was just like stepping off into nothing. I remember getting a couple of addresses and things, but those kids too were in flux.

Julia

When I found out I was having to leave the States to go to New Delhi at the age of 13, I was very upset! And unlike Yugoslavia, I remained upset. We took a long, slow trip to get to India, all across Europe, northern Africa, the Middle East and I remember fighting every step of the way, crying, being angry. I remained terribly upset.

It evaporated -- I remember the precise moment when my anger evaporated -- when the plane came into New Delhi for its landing and looking out the window I could see the small green patches of land and the circling of the bullocks. I could see small figures running out onto the tarmac with monsoon umbrellas to greet the plane.

But I didn't want to start all over again. I had really worked at becoming a popular girl at my old school. I had gone from the dowdy kid in gray to becoming one of the most popular. It was a fairly quick transition, but I had adjusted.

Andy

People always ask me how it was to move around so much as a kid, and I tell them `It was all I knew.' It was like another adventure, `Oh, boy -- a new place.' I looked on it rather positively. I don't think it occurred to me -- I was in eighth grade -- that I would be losing my Japanese friends, my riding privileges....

From Jerusalem on, I always had to be aware of other people watching me and trying to figure out what their rules were. I sometimes wonder about all the uprooting. It seemed so easy -- then. But I'm realizing now that it probably was harder than I let on to myself.

Barbara

I think you always feel grief at leaving. The main way I expressed it, and I still express it today, is by -- we usually knew about six months before that we were moving but even if it was only a week -- we'd spend that last chunk of time seeing all the problems we'd had in that country, or culture, and being really happy to leave it for those reasons. Also we'd be really excited about the new things we could move on to. You leave those old problems -- that horrible teacher -- behind and thank goodness that next year you could be in a totally different atmosphere and start all over. That's how it happens.

Marooned!

<u>Sarah</u>

My brother and I were sent out of Sierra Leone together at about the ages of ten and eight to a Swiss boarding school. Most of the other kids in the school were in similar circumstances, with parents all over the world. This school separation was very hard. That was certainly the hardest separation. But it didn't occur to us that we couldn't do it, or that we could change it. The school was very small, 32 students in K through 8th grade. We were in just one building, a Swiss chalet.

We felt more secure knowing each other was there, but we didn't spend a lot of time together. Only one particular incident stands out. I remember the time I got a letter from Mom telling about the death of our beloved dog and Tony and I sat by each other on the stairs to the basement, where the lockers, showers and two classrooms were, and we cried together. We'd lost our little dog, Hector. That was the only time we were really together there. After only about five minutes for that exchange of grief, we were back to what we were supposed to be doing. We had finished eating and we all had little lockers downstairs and it was in the time allotment we had between the dining room and getting downstairs to change that we had this moment of grief together.... I remember sitting on the stairs and people were walking over us and by us. I think it was symbolic, and the whole thing of being alone, and the other kids were also under very similar circumstances....

<u>Tony</u>

One of the hardest things was when I began (at) Deerfield I didn't have a known "home." My parents had spent the summer on home leave before going off to Curacao and they settled the house there without either of us children. I had no sense of having a room somewhere, somewhere where my things were and an identification with "home." It wasn't until I went home at Christmas that it was sorted out, although my mother did send me a complete set of photos depicting the house and grounds and major rooms, including mine. At Christmas I could finally see where the familiar bits had been placed, a rug here, that chair there, my bed, etc.

Christine

That was a hard time for me, especially being sort of alone, or I felt alone because my parents weren't with me. In a way I felt orphaned, I thought about that a lot. I also felt like I was the one who had to hold the family together. I think I was the most sane of them. I think a part of me just understood that this is just the way life is, and you can either suffer or you can just move on and carry what you know with you and not let it fester. I think, maybe it was because of my age, or maybe because I was just more flexible, but I could adapt. And I forced myself; I wanted to become like everybody else because I didn't want to be an outsider any more.

Andrea

Then I went to college. There had been some talk in the spring about my parents going to Czechoslovakia. My mom said we would get a horse, because she'd always said that if they went to Eastern Europe she would get a horse. She loved to ride and that would be cheaper there. Right -- that was the carrot because she didn't want to go to Eastern Europe. She knew she didn't want to go there. But what happened instead is that they went to Somalia.

They left in October. They dropped me off at college in Connecticut and a month later they took off. They had been living in D.C. So they left. That summer I went to Somalia to see them and did some stuff there. The next year -- that next summer -- I traveled.

I met friends in between vacations. I met some college friends in Paris, and I had a boyfriend that I met up with in Luxembourg and we hitch-hiked and camped.

I came back to the States later that summer and worked at a camp for emotionally disturbed kids. Things started getting rough -- for me. I started having some trouble. I basically fell apart, a nervous breakdown or whatever you want to call it. I was taking care of these kids and it was a very high stress kind of situation. I guess it must have been because of that. They were basically inner-city New York kids. I had a couple that were really messed up, retarded and helpless. I don't know, maybe it was just ready to happen.

By that point my parents were back in the States. The camp counselor thought he could help me at first, but I was pretty out of it. He finally called my parents and they came up and got an ambulance to take me back to D.C. They gave me some medication and then I was fine, but I ended up needing a certain amount of psychiatric care. It was while I was going through all that -- being in the hospital for a while -- that I was telling things to my parents. Right when they brought me back, when it was still pretty acute, I was flooded with all these things from the Foreign Service times. A lot of things from Moscow. Memories. I told my parents about all these things I'd never told them before. People climbing the gate and those kinds of things.

I ended up being in therapy for a while and I got a chance to talk about all these things I hadn't had a chance to talk about. I think it was fortunate that my parents were in the country when this happened. I did feel I was on my own when they went to Somalia. That was hard. I guess I just ... you think by college (age) you should feel fine, and in some ways I did. But in other ways, if I ever wanted any advice or anything from them, it took so long to get anything back. I did write them. At that time you couldn't call or telegram Somalia. We relied on the mail, and it took a month. By that time you've gotten over whatever it is. I think it was just not having anybody to talk to really.

I don't really feel close to my parents now. I don't know. It's funny -- if I really wasn't talking to them that much anyway, it shouldn't make a difference. But somehow it was different. Just knowing that if you really didn't like the situation you were in, there was a home. All of a sudden it was as if I had no home. It didn't feel like home being in the dorm. It feels so strange at first. And there was no home in D.C. because there is nothing there. It's been rented out -- there's no family there. They are in some country you haven't even been to. It's not even a place you know. All your stuff is in storage somewhere; you'll never get to see it for umpteen million years.

Minority Status -- The Realities of Them and Us

Craig

Religion opens up a whole new arena because for the first time in my life I was exposed to anti-Semitism overseas. In addition to going through this mobility, I was usually the only Jewish person. That was very difficult because I wanted to fit in so badly. I was very reluctant to tell anybody I was Jewish. I used to dread Christmas. People would ask me what religion I was and I would deny being of any religion. You only had a small group to fit into! Where are you going to go? Comments would be made, I would hear things. People didn't know I was Jewish, and that was painful. I never confronted my parents with that. I think I made it difficult, also, it just added to the stress of moving around so much.

... I think they expected me to be that nice Jewish boy that maybe I would have been had I stayed in this country -- I probably would have come out fairly stereotypical. But I wasn't exposed to it. I think when I came back from overseas, they expected me to resort back to that. But I didn't know how. I didn't know any Jews overseas. None of my friends were Jewish. So maybe you could say I was in a culture within a culture.

I never had a barmitzvah. While we were in Morocco my father tried to get some guy to give me Hebrew classes over the weekend, but I resisted and finally he gave up. I think I've dated one Jewish girl in my life, and that was a disaster. I've never had any interest in religion. The last time I attended a synagogue service, I was eight years old.

Andy

I finished eighth grade in Saudi, I was 13. It was a great experience in many ways. There was an American Air Force base down the road that the U.S. had built right after World War II. There was a very small number of Americans stationed there, but they had a swimming pool. The consulate was a little compound on the desert. Two miles down the road was the oil company compound -- Aramco. One square mile of land behind a barbed wire fence and inside was American suburbia. There was a movie theater there, I had friends who lived there. They had their own school which we were not allowed to participate in. It was sort of weird in that way. I felt a lot of resentment at being "ghettoized" -- you could have this privilege, but you can't have that. I became aware of the privileges and status I had, the child of a Foreign Service Officer. I didn't like it ... I think I became aware. In a way I think it politicized me, in the same way that someone at a young age could become aware of class differences.

For instance, about a mile from our house was a horse stable run by Aramco people where I would walk every day after school. And there were these beautiful Arabian horses and they needed someone to exercise them. So I really got into horseback riding and became pretty good at it. They didn't pay me to do this, but I became a jockey for a number of horses I exercised. I entered them into the competitions they were running -- Texas barrel racing, pole bending, and also English show riding and gymkhana stuff, where a whole lot of horses go through elaborate routines. One day I was in gymkhana practice with the rest of the team and there was a woman in the stadium who called over to our instructor and insisted that her son get a place on the team and said "Take that consulate kid off because he's not really one of us!" My instructor felt compelled to do it. I grew up thinking, actually, that I was sort of privileged, in a Foreign Service surrounding; there were servants, there was this black passport you could sort of wave at people, and your daddy drove around in a car with a flag on it. And yet suddenly, in Saudi Arabia, they had the privileges and I didn't, or they were taken away from me. It was bizarre. The rationale was that the oil company had paid to set up this elaborate stable.

I continued to ride and just before leaving Saudi Arabia I won a clean sweep of all their horseback trophies. A little personal victory!

After ... home leave ... we moved to Bombay, India. My parents had the choice of sending me to the American School in New Delhi or to one of the two mission schools -- Woodstock or Kodaikanal. They'd heard some good things about Kodai, so they sent me there.

During (my) Outward Bound (experience) I'd grown a beard, and I really liked it. My parents said, "Well, it's a missionary school and we've been told you aren't allowed to have a beard, so you should shave it." So I did. I got there and I was assigned to live not on campus in a dormitory but in a house off campus with a bunch of other kids who all came from a particular Lutheran mission in India. There was a house father, and the first thing he did was to take all my Beatles tapes and erase them and put hymn music on them. Part of the routine was up at 6 AM, cold showers -- really cold showers -- there was no heat at 8,000 feet. It was cold and it was January.

It was a very foreign experience to be surrounded by ... these were kids who, some of them, had been plucked out of Oklahoma and sent overseas. One of my first roommates -- after a month when I finally got out of the house and into a dormitory -- was this kid who'd never been outside Oklahoma before, a born-again Christian whose father was a preacher. He was the kind of kid that on weekends would get on a soapbox and preach on the street corners in downtown

Tulsa, or wherever. He was a nice country boy, a nice guy, easy to get along with, and we'd stay up late at night arguing religion. It was a wonderful experience in some ways and I formed very, very close friendships.... Ninety percent of these kids were sons and daughters of missionaries. Some of them were from missionary families going back generations in India, or China....

Julia

When I was in Yugoslavia it was during years of building and optimism. I do remember though, even as a child, how the servants were often angry or afraid. In Yugoslavia we as children were close to the servants, they were a big part of our lives. I was a child and we were often left in their care. Also I was a girl, which meant I could be treated with physical closeness by the women, hugged and kissed and held on their laps. By contrast, in India there were only men working in the household and in that culture you are set apart sexually by the time you are seven or eight, or even earlier. I would never have been picked up or given a hug as I was in Yugoslavia. So my relationship with the servants in India was much more distant then that of my brother, who was younger and, being male, was treated more normally by the servants. Also in Yugoslavia the servants lived in the house right there with us. I spent a lot of time visiting in the servants' rooms, sitting on the bed, where we talked and I was told stories. Whereas in India they had their own quarters and families.

Gail

In India we had some servants, a chauffeur and an ayah and people like that. I think that -- although I have no memory of it -- it was probably painful to leave them. When we came back years later they were all there at the train station platform to meet us. My parents had kept in touch with them, so obviously it was a good relationship. But in Ghana we had servants, but one of them started paying attention to me because I was turning into a 12 year-old girl and it was becoming very uncomfortable. I was just glad to get out of there.... I always felt really uncomfortable with the servants because of the difference in class and poverty and all that.

Andrea

My dad was working really long hours. For vacations we waited until we had home leave. I shouldn't say that though. We went on picnics -- my parents are real big on picnics. You get into the car, you pack up this food, and you go exploring somewhere. We used to stop by the side of the road. We used to do this in Garmisch too, we always did this. Except that it was a lot more fun in Germany. In Russia, the hard part was that you weren't supposed to stop your car, and you get in trouble if you go into various places, so you had to be really careful where you stopped. Then, when we would stop, as soon as we sat down to eat, a ring of people would collect and stare at us. It was very uncomfortable. When Dad was there, he was able to be kind of joking, talkative and lively, and eventually I would still be aware they were there but it wasn't terrible. But if it was just my mom and us, I think she had the same feeling we did, that it was kind of creepy. And you felt uncomfortable. It was blank staring (and) they wouldn't look away. It was like we were just really strange -- like zoo animals.

Maybe I Should Have Just Stayed Home

<u>Christine</u>

I think when I came back to go to school after Korea I was focussed on just fitting in. I didn't have a sense of loss -- I do now. I wish that I hadn't been that way. I feel like I've lost my identity now, because I forced myself to adapt. I'm angry about that and I'm guilty about that. I don't think I was my own person. I think if I had been, I wouldn't have cared what other people thought. I wanted to be more like my brothers -- I wish I'd been more like the friends I know of now who were like that. I don't know if they are any happier than I am, but certainly they have much simpler lives, which is what I kind of want. But, I'll always feel different; there will always be that background. It makes me feel special, too. I treasure that.

<u>Craig</u>

I had no concept of my identity whatsoever as a youngster. Probably not until I was about 35. From the time I came back to the U.S. to finish high school -- or even throughout the time I was overseas -- until I was about 35, I never had any idea who I was. I was dragged from one place to another. Leaving friends had created a tremendous amount of insecurity on my part.... My feelings were really secondary when we were overseas. I did voice concerns many times, like, "Gee, I wish I was back in the States. Why don't you put me into boarding school?" But I never outright refused to go.

I did go back to my old house in Philadelphia, the one that we lived in before we started going overseas. That was very nostalgic. I was very happy there until we left. I had a normal childhood, a normal life. I had local friends who were my neighbors -- I was very happy.

If I had to do my life all over again I think I would prefer to just have a regular childhood, like anybody else, like most people. There is plenty of time to travel in your lifetime. I think that would have made me much more secure. I think that would be the biggest difference. I'm still very insecure, but not as bad as I was. It's good to have roots, it's good to know who your relatives are, it's good to have friends who are around you from grade school, through high school.

You can never revert to the "typical American kid" after being overseas -- it isn't going to happen. Rootlessness takes over.

CHAPTER EIGHT

WHAT HINDERED, WHAT HELPED,
HOW I FEEL ABOUT IT ALL NOW

Introduction

Every family approaches transitions in its own way and every family member evolves ways of coping. That said, it is pretty obvious that families find it difficult, if not impossible, to meet all the needs of individual members during any one international move. The employee member or members are preoccupied with professional leave-taking and then reestablishing again as soon as they arrive at a new destination or posting. Someone usually is in charge of the logistical parts -- the packing, cleaning, unpacking, the survival skills needed in any new cultural setting. School age children face the task of leaving old friends, making new friends, adapting to a new school and home. Often schedules change dramatically from place to place. At the last post maybe everyone gathered daily for a lunch made and served by household employees followed by a mid-day nap; at the new place Dad leaves at seven in the morning to start a long commute, and demanding social obligations prevent Mom and Dad from having either lunch or dinner with their children most days during the week. Family life often gets caught up in "the luck of the draw."

At the same time, individuals within a family usually don't have a clue how other family members are feeling about a move. The "stiff upper lip" approach prevailed within the voices' families. Everyone was on their own to sort out their emotions. No one probed deeply enough to see if anyone was feeling grief, resentment, anxiousness; yet it is impossible to think that everyone within a family facing such a move didn't have those feelings, parents and children alike. The work of any relocation still seems to be more busy work than head work.

Given all the variables, some aspects of every move are similar to all the others. There are some actions parents can take that will help children through the transition. There are some things that the children will learn to do for themselves which will make it easier on them. For example, the matter of pets. Many of the voices mentioned how grateful they were that pets went with them from post to post. In some families it was not even an issue worth considering, it was just a given. Parents can also try to give children some degree of self-determination within the decision-making process. Even though most of the voices saw that their input was a sham, they appreciated being consulted, being informed. Parents can work harder to place their children in appropriate schools, at appropriate levels, and take an interest in those schools and teachers. All the voices seemed to have a "school from Hell" story.

Parents should try to offer accurate information about a new place, for the good and bad. The carrot and stick method of enticement -- "when you get to ..., you can learn to sail" -- may make things worse if the parent finds it difficult or impossible to deliver on such a promise. Besides, everyone has benchmarks and expectations based on their own experiences, even children. They have to be allowed to develop their own sensory skills, to learn through their own situations.

While most of the voices experienced some measure of violence overseas, they looked on it as an adventure rather than a frightening situation. A lot of credit for that goes to their parents who were not folding under pressure or frightening their children. One perception reinforced through the violence -- one the voices learned very early in their internationally mobile childhoods -- was that they did live on the surface. Neither they nor their parents were in any way responsible for whatever was happening around them.

As the voices assessed their legacies as internationally mobile children, most of them readily acknowledged that it was a wonderful life. For most, the gains balance the losses, they treasure their understanding of a larger world, and they feel resilient and able to adapt to most anything.

THE VOICES

A Small Voice May Be Better Than No Voice At All

Andy

My parents would sort of go through the pretense -- I realize it was a pretense -- that I had a choice. They would sit me down and they'd say, "Well, what would you think about going to Cairo next year?" I'd realize I had no choice but.... They explained to me often that there wasn't a whole lot of choice for them either. When their tour was up they had to move someplace else within these narrow options. It was clear to me that I was anywhere for a certain length of time. But to a kid, two years is a long time. I guess that made it easier to think about leaving when the time came.

Andrea

... I have no recollection how I found out we were going to Garmisch. Later on I have a recollection. I think that my parents were pretty straight with us in terms of letting us know when they knew, but they didn't have a lot of notice. A couple of times they thought we were going somewhere and then it would change.

Peter

My being able to choose how and where I did my alternative service again says something about how our family operated. There was the sense that forces that were bigger than me and beyond my control did dictate certain things about my life, and what we did or what we had to do. But within that, I always had a sense of making that mine too, embracing it. This was very much the same. Yes, I had to do my service, but I had the status that I had chosen because I felt it was the right status to have. And then I volunteered to do it, rather than to go to college just then. So that was a choice I made, a control that I had.

Gail

Ours was a family where the adults told the children what to do -- we weren't brought into any of the decision making about assignments. It was very funny because my whole family was together in London this summer for a week, and we hadn't been together as a family in years and years. It was fascinating to see how we all dropped back into our little roles in the family. I was the good little girl and I kept my mouth shut and was quiet. My brother was arrogant and know-it-all. And my sister was the rebel and jokester. I saw us all as being even more-so of what we were before. But what my father saw was "Gee, this is terrible. This is no longer a dictatorship. I'm in the middle of a democracy now. This isn't fun anymore!" It was so very clear. We were telling him what we were doing. He was used to planning everything. He was no longer running the show. That was quite a shock in terms of the changing family dynamics. Whenever we traveled together we were children and parents. We had never traveled together as a group of adults in those roles.

Sally

... before our move to Mexico I remember sitting on the porch at some friends and Mom or Dad said, "How would you feel about moving to Mexico?" And I said, "I don't want to go!" It was always pretty much a done deal by the time I came into the equation. I was powerless and I didn't have any input. But I don't think it's up to the children to say where the parents go. At that point in my life that was appropriate.

Craig

I didn't feel like I was a participant in the moving process. Absolutely not. When it came close to the time my father would be reassigned, we would anxiously anticipate the decision. He would say there's a chance we might go here or there, but beyond that, I was not involved in the decision making process. He would tell us the places we might go.... Once the decision was made, we packed and moved.... I would tell parents today to involve their kids in the decision-making process. I had no say in the matter.

We Built Our Character and Learned to Adapt!

Michael

My parents never came to me and said, "This is what we're going to do." But it wouldn't be put to me as a question (like) "Do you want to do this?" Instead it was couched in terms of how it might make me happy. The bottom line I felt was always, "The decision has been made and I'm going to have to go along with it." Each time, as I got older, I fought it a little harder, although I always knew in the back of my mind that each time it got easier in another sense. The leaving got harder each time but the adaptation to the new place got easier.

Craig

I think Foreign Service kids are very adaptable, I think that's the thing that sets us apart from other children. But being adaptive and being happy and comfortable are two different things -- they don't always go hand in hand. Yeah, I'm flexible. You can put me anywhere and I'll probably adjust somehow, that's the way I was brought up.

Andy

That summer that we were evacuated from Cairo and went on home leave was very unusual.... My father enrolled me in Outward Bound so I did a four week course in survival training. It was an experience and I really got a lot out of it, although I hated it at times. It required a lot of endurance. I was just turning 16 and I came out of it thinking I could do anything. I'm sure it helped ease me back into America when I came back for college two years later. There were no other kids there with my background. About a quarter of the kids had been picked out of the ghettos of Detroit and Newark -- they were black -- where that summer there were soldiers camped in their front yards and on their streets. These kids had never been outside their cities, much less in the wilderness. In that situation everyone was reduced to a common denominator and it was all about surviving and getting your food, and getting to the campfire before all the food was gone. You had to defend yourself and be sure others didn't encroach on your territory and your food and equipment. It was all very basic. They tried to emphasize both cooperation and individualism. They broke you up into teams as part of a patrol, and there was some silly little motto which emphasized "to serve and not to yield." A lot of it involved learning how to push yourself and how not to give up under all the physical pain. Then in the end you did learn that you had to ultimately depend on other people in a bad situation. Some of these kids were fat and physically not able to maintain the pace of the stronger ones, and at one point our patrol picked a leader who was very strong physically and he set a pace that pushed it too far. He turned out to have a mean streak in him as well -- he liked pushing. Some of us eventually led a revolt and deposed him. When I read Lord of the Flies in high school, I identified!

In this Outward Bound situation, my background and where I was from really didn't matter so much. I quickly realized that what was important for me was to form the right alliances with people I could trust and who would help me survive this little experience.

Julia

One thing I would like to say. Most of what, in my experience, I think of as being fabulous, a wonderful treasure and a continuing source of a lot of strength, intellectual enjoyment, all kinds of things -- the one issue that has remained as I've gotten older and matured, and one thing I haven't really conquered, has to do with the down side of the ability to adapt. I became aware that I was too good at adapting, that I could fit into any crowd very quickly and effectively, no matter what kind of a group it was. Privately I would hold back and have a lot of private judgments about it but not discuss them and after a while I began to realize that this was dishonest. For example in a professional setting, rather than challenge -- mind you, I worked for the Senate -- I became very skillful at figuring out how to advance my agenda using language and concepts they would respond to. To some extent that's a good thing to know. But after a certain point it becomes manipulative and dishonest. I've stated it at its most extreme. But I began to be aware at some point in my late 20s that I needed to be careful. I was too good at it. It's not that I ever did anything I'm ashamed of but I began to wonder what the psychic process was in not being direct.

The second related thing is a hatred of confrontation. Part of this relates to the cultures we lived in. For example in polite society in India the greatest challenge to courtesy is to receive a gift because as recipient you have to make the giver feel worthy. Giving a gift is not considered particularly challenging. I find it very difficult to point to someone and say "Don't do it that way, do it this way." I've learned to do it, but in a work situation it can be really difficult and that concerns me. I've found other ways of getting what I want but it doesn't seem as ethical as just saying `no, this is wrong.' I have a couple of very close foreign service friends -- one I know quite well but others who I don't know as well -- but for everybody this seems to be "the issue." You are so trained to put yourself in the other person's shoes! It takes a while for people to realize it, getting to your 30s. It's a destructive side of this life. This is a legacy that's not so attractive. I think I became aware of it because I was in politics and I was in the business of trying to get people through varying degrees to do something differently. For me it was a moral issue. So I had to do a lot of thinking about how do you do that. What's acceptable. How far can you go. At its most extreme, it becomes dishonest -- to yourself. I think that the dishonesty does a disservice not only to yourself but to the values you grew up with.

A simpler way of saying this is that we all verge on glibness. We're just too good at adapting. When I was a youngster trying to cope with the traumas of moving around, the thing I remember trying to do consciously was fit in. What I've tried to do as an adult, consciously, is to draw lines to challenge, confront. It's exactly the opposite. I can quickly meld into a group, they will think that I am a part of it, but I will be holding out, making judgments. They may not know it and I am thinking to myself -- now in my 40s -- if I don't entirely feel comfortable with everything about this group's culture and mores, I may not adopt those things. I may either adapt passively, or slip out the door.

Hit or Miss Educational Systems

<u>Sally</u>

I went to a regular public school in England, a very small school in the village of Kimpton. Then at the end of fifth grade I went to St. Alban's Grammar School for Girls. I wasn't the only American then. There was one other American girl. I went through the British school system. I think when I went to the St. Alban's Grammar School for Girls, I don't know if this was even a consideration, but there was an American School in London but I would have had to take an hour long train ride to get into London every day. I was perfectly happy where I was. I don't think there was any need for me to move to an American school.

When I went to Mexico I was tested with some California aptitude test when I was in eighth grade. I took reading, writing and arithmetic and my lowest score showed I was doing math at the tenth grade level and I was reading at the thirteenth grade level. My English schooling prepared me well.

<u>Michael</u>

My high school years were split. I was here in Washington for ninth and started tenth, and then in October we moved to Bonn, West Germany, so I finished tenth grade in Bonn in a Department of Defense school which only went up to tenth grade. Then I had to make a decision about where to go after that. That was an agonizing experience because all my friends were going through the same thing -- much like seniors in high school go through searching for a college. The difference was that we all had first and foremost in our minds to try and find a place where we could all go together, and yet, unlike college, ultimately our parents were going to make the decision, not us. I can remember of my three closest friends, all of us had focussed on going to an international school in The Hague, which had a boarding section. Of these three friends, one was German, but he had an American mother and that's why he was in the Defense school. His parents wanted to put him in a German school. The other two were relatively open as to where they could go; our parents figured we should go to another international English language school and not a German school since it would be for only two years. They felt it would be a disadvantage for us not knowing the language. We were all interested in this school in The Hague and we visited it, and my other two friends decided to go there. Then my parents came up with this other option of going to school in Geneva where they had a close friend who could keep an eye on me. We made an arrangement where I took a room in her apartment. Ultimately going to Geneva made the most sense. It was a better school and my parents had friends there and the boarding situation was better. Yet my other friends were going to school in The Hague and I was really torn about that. But in the end I decided on Geneva -- hard to tell if it was my decision, but my parents made me feel like I made the decision. I often wonder if I'd opted the other way, which wasn't their choice, who would have won out?

I went to Geneva for eleventh grade. Before I finished eleventh grade my parents moved back to Washington. That created a whole new dilemma -- would I come back to the United States and finish my senior year? I didn't want to do that for my last year, and also I'd be a lot farther away from my family. It wouldn't have been easy to shuttle back and forth for the holidays or for weekends. At that time the education allowances weren't as good as they are today, but it wouldn't have mattered anyway. Finally, fortunately, my high school guidance counselor came up with this brilliant idea that I had enough credits to graduate a year early. In all the shifting of schools, so many new schools, I guess I was lucky that it all added up. I was in something like an advanced placement program, so that gave me almost all the extra credits I needed. I needed only one more credit to graduate from high school a year early. I finished up in Geneva and came back to Washington and took one course in summer school and finished. That whole plan was developed at the last minute so I hadn't applied to college or anything. At that stage, it was just finish a year early and then take a year off before going to college. It worked out well. I worked here in Washington during that year in a Senator's office.

Barbara

I arrived in Cyprus when I was ten. I went to a very strict, British Catholic school in Cyprus. That was hard. I went from being the smartest kid in my class to being the dumbest kid in that class. The British learn everything by memory and rote; they are very polite, I had to wear a uniform, we all had to wear our hair back, we had Mass every morning for the first half hour, we all had to stand in single-file lines. The school was for both boys and girls, but they were separated. We had a headmaster and a headmistress. We did the Mass together -- the boys would be on one end of the room and we'd be on the other.

They did things so differently. I wasn't used to learning by memorization because Americans learn more by experience, at least at that time. They were very strict. Whenever the teacher came in we all had to stand up and say "Good morning, Mrs. Hagdjanickaloy" -- or whatever. Just little things would be a problem. I'd be mumbling and they'd think I was talking back to them and I'd be called up to the front of the room and my hand would be whipped with a ruler, and things like that. It was a junior school. The teachers were all British or British married to Cypriots, like Mrs. H....   She was a real spark-plug of a lady; she was like a drill sergeant. She put the fear of life into us. She was our English teacher and we used to have to memorize a poem each week. I remember one time in particular I had to memorize "The Fly" by Robert Louis Stevenson. She would pick us randomly to recite our poems, if we didn't recite it correctly she would really tear us apart in front of the class. I was much more interested in doing other things. I had always been an outdoors person and so I always forgot to memorize my poem until about 15 minutes before class. Oh, she put the fear of God in me! I remember a lot of what she taught me, though. Actually it was a very good school.

My parents really wanted me to be in the American educational system so I could go to America for college. Even though the European/British school system from age 10 to 18 is probably better than the American, they felt the American universities were much better than the European. They also didn't want me to have to go through those tests, (the) A and O levels. They thought that was too much pressure on a child and could hurt me.

Andy

I was four years old when we moved to Jerusalem. That was a two year assignment. I have memories of it, but they are sort of hazy. I was there from four to six. I started school there in an Arabic language school in East Jerusalem. The city was then divided. This was a school run by Franciscan Brothers, I believe. Every academic quarter the language of instruction would change; the first quarter was Arabic, the second was French, the third was English. I lasted the first trisect. It was not a great experience, in fact it was very traumatic. I was the only American in the class -- there was one other British kid -- and this was during a period of heightened political tensions in Jerusalem because Nasser was rising very fast.

I have vivid memories of that school and fighting to stay out of the school bus. They had to cram me in every morning. I did learn quite a bit of Arabic, but I just didn't adapt to it. It was a rote method of learning. If you gave the wrong answer you had to hold out your hand and the teacher would smack you with the ruler. It was pretty awful. I fought it and they eventually transferred me to a British School in West Jerusalem. Every morning I would have to cross over through Mandelbaum Gate in a diplomatic car, weaving in and out of the tank barriers. There were a few American kids being taken across like that. It wasn't dangerous, but I have memories of it sort of feeling dangerous. The Jordanians would search the car and they had guns, then the Israelis would ... it was all so foreign. I became very aware that the passions and the violence that surrounded us were real issues.

Rob

The first difficult period for me I guess was going to a nursery school and having an out of body experience. I was going to a school I didn't want to go to. I felt confined. There was a French school ... in Haifa. My problem was that it was the only school geared for my age group.... I remember I felt I was in a bubble; I did not speak French, everyone else did. I guess I must not have conversed because they did send me to French class. I remember just sitting there and just watching motions and movements, but not understanding a word.

When I was 12 I went to a British school in Ealing called St. Benedicts. We had to wear uniforms, gray wool. I was two years at St. Benedicts, from '62 to '64, and then one year ... my father decided -- this is fun -- that I was ready for high school. I was only in the (seventh) grade, I wasn't in high school. I think he lost track of what grade I was in because he enrolled me in Canterbury Prep School in Canterbury, Connecticut. He was afraid that if I stayed in a British school I wouldn't matriculate to the point where I would be accepted into an institution of higher learning in the States. He didn't want to send me to the DOD (Department of Defense) school, he felt it was inferior. Maybe he thought there was a difference in my chronological age. So basically I skipped eighth grade when he sent me back to Connecticut to boarding school. My father felt that since I had gone to a British school for two years I was probably farther ahead than my American colleagues. But I wasn't farther ahead and it was more uprooting, if anything. I felt that being plucked out of St. Benedicts in Ealing was more disruptive to my education than anything else. I did not do well at all. I didn't take my schooling seriously. I was having too much fun meeting people. I was unhappy and wound up going back to England. I didn't feel ostracized socially by the kids at Canterbury. I just wasn't academically prepared. What I had learned prior to that was sort of a hodge-podge -- new math, old math -- I had no structured primary education. Most of my education took place outside the classroom. And even when I went to St. Benedicts in Ealing, I was with students who had been in an institution from the lower grades right up. The British place a great deal of importance on primary education, because they often leave school at 16.

I got to England at a time when they had something called the "eleven plus" which was just devastating to a lot of families. At that time the kids took a test at eleven years old that determined whether (they) were going on to an institution of higher learning or not. I remember the devastation that some of the parents of my classmates felt when the students didn't pass the eleven plus. I think it was abolished the year after I left. I thought it was just awful; not only that, I think it's an act of discrimination. That was my first feeling, that everybody ought to have an opportunity or a chance. One thing that is great about America is that they hold out for late bloomers, we always have a chance. I was shocked by this test system in England.

I came back after that year in Connecticut and went to the Department of Defense school, Central High School, and I had a great time, I enjoyed it. But again, I didn't take academics that seriously. Two areas I enjoyed were English and history, and that was about it. Everything else didn't seem applicable, it didn't help me. And there was no sense of importance placed on these subjects. I think that reflected the teachers who were teaching in this system. There were some teachers who genuinely cared about the process of imparting knowledge, but there were those who were there for the ride, so to speak.

It was not a warm and fuzzy institution. They followed a set curriculum and activities, approved and sanctioned by the DOD or the NEA, or whatever.... And actually my dad had a valid argument. It wasn't the most academically inspired institution. It was the cookie cutter approach, it was the factory model school. In at nine and out by three -- boom. We shuffled from one class to the next and if it was one o'clock it was time for lunch.

One thing I feel very strongly about for my children is a cohesive education. I think aspects of my education did suffer. Especially my math skills, my analytical skills. I'm not a good number man. With respect to primary education, I think it's important to have some stability. I think that's what I'm trying to do with my children. If later, when they are in high school and we move, well, then that's fine. Through the eighth grade it is really important to get those basic skills. My primary education was so fragmented in terms of my math and science. I went from old math to new math, right into geometry. The British have an entirely different system.

Peter

I did my high school by correspondence through the American School of Chicago. In some ways that did compromise my social life as a teenager. We were living up in the mountains, I was living in a community of Koreans. There weren't any other kids my age, even Korean kids. The nearest house was almost a mile away. The village there was strung out along the highway. I did not get to know the people in the community very well because we were so far away. My whole life was centered right there at the Abbey.

When I came back from Korea I stayed with my aunt in Boone, North Carolina. I was finishing up high school. I was 19. I took an extra year to do my high school because of the way I was doing it by correspondence. I'd do a little bit here, a little bit there, then go off and do some traveling, then come back, then something else ... I'd be doing my lessons on the hillside enjoying the sun more than I was doing my lesson, stuff like that. I did my lessons totally on my own. The correspondence school was designed mainly for adults who were working on getting their high school diplomas. I think we had to get special permission because I was not an adult. My father had Calvert home schooling when he was a little kid. That's where the parents teach the child....

Christine

I thought the education I got was horrible. I used it as an excuse to not want to learn. I would go to the teachers and say, "I just moved here, we didn't study this in my old school. I don't want to learn that -- I'm in music." I was never forced. It wasn't a good education. I resent that now. My classes were small, they were unorganized. I'm sure all the teachers had seen kids come and go, and come and go; they knew we were just going to go off to some other school somewhere and learn something else. I think that bothers me the most these days, the education. I certainly got "life education" and I got to see the cultures and that's invaluable. But schooling was different. The sense of having any standard kind of curriculum was missing.

When I got to college I had to try hard. I think harder than a lot of people. But I didn't feel too (far) behind. I really wanted to learn at that point. I took psychology, English, technical writing, then I had my artistic areas. I knew that to do anything that I really wanted to do -- like I thought seriously about being a psychologist -- I didn't have all the proper courses or education for it. I would have to start at the very beginning. That intimidated me, so I just never attempted it. I never took biology, I never took algebra, I never took trigonometry. I never took any of those things. Kids here would have to do that. In that sense I've always felt like I've been fighting to ... partly to not let anybody know, employers, and just struggling very hard to do the work without having that background. I think I've come a long way with it and I'm proud of myself in that respect. But a lot of it is that I didn't try when I was younger.

Craig

In the eighth grade I went to three schools. Our home leave occurred during September and October of that year and my father didn't want me to miss any school, so I was in school in the United States for a period of about a month before we left for Cambodia. The year was 1963. It was probably about the most difficult period of all. Actually during the eighth grade I was in three different schools, in three different countries; the United States during home leave, then Cambodia, and then to Bolivia. There were a lot of schools and a lot of different countries. I think that is one of the hardest things for a kid to experience -- going from one school to another, trying to make friends, having to leave friends. In the United States it is very difficult, particularly in junior high. Kids that age are very, very insensitive.

Of Family and Home Bases

Sarah

We had a place of reference that seemed like home all during our childhood. Our paternal grandmother's big rambling home in Santa Barbara -- where our Dad had been born -- was a place of comfortable disorder where we stayed with our cousins during the summers. It was always a place where we were at home on the spur of the moment. And there was always room for more. Sometimes there were as many as 20 to 30 of us gathering there. We slept anywhere -- the sleeping porch, living room, anywhere. We even kept chalked marks up in the attic to mark our growth. From year to year nothing changed, we'd find the chalk in the same place we'd left it.

Our Grandmother, Cookie -- my name for her -- was our family and gave us a sense of place. Now our uncle has the house and it has become a showplace, not at all a place of welcome. The chalk marks were removed, everything has been made over, remodeled. I still regret losing this anchor. It would almost have been easier if it had been bought by someone outside the family.

Gail

I see my parents a lot. They are much a part of my daughter's life. I really wanted that. I saw how I hardly knew my grandparents at all. My last surviving grandmother came to live with us in India for a couple of years and we just had no connection with each other. She was very elderly and not in good health at that time. I was a teenager and off doing my own thing. I felt perennially guilty after that for not spending more time with her. She was ensconced in her air-conditioned room, and wouldn't mix with the servants, had a hard time and sort of isolated herself in a sense. I saw how my mother ... we had just arrived in Ghana when she got the news that her mother had died and her father died while she was overseas, and my father's father died while we were overseas. My mother told me she never had a sense of closure about those deaths because it was like they had never really happened. She read about it in a letter....

Relatives to us were always benevolent strangers that we saw every two years. I got to know one of my aunts that year that I lived in Illinois. She became sort of my surrogate mother. We had a lot in common and a wonderful relationship. But that was the first time I ever got to really know my relatives. I really made an emotional connection with my aunt. I'd spend holidays with them, and she'd call me at school and say that I should call her at any time, reverse the charges. It was so comforting to me to have her available.

Craig

I was very close to my mother's parents, and that was very difficult because I never really got to spend much time with them during those years overseas. That too is difficult. That's another thing. I have cousins today who if I saw them on the street, I probably wouldn't recognize them because I had so little contact with them. I don't know where they are, who is alive and who is not alive. My parents never talk about them. I really never got to know many of my relatives or cousins. I had no sense of family stability growing up.

CHAPTER NINE

WHAT STUCK -- EVALUATIONS AND WISHES

Introduction

As individuals we often wonder what it is that forms us; where we get our strengths, if we can ever overcome our weaknesses, why we react as we do in certain situations. Some may say our star sign or rank order within a family might have more to do with the way we are than factors like geographical mobility. Certainly parents are the biggest influence in our lives. We share their genetic codes and they are our first mentors. But life experience is made up of many different parts. How we experience what we experience, and how that is processed long term really is key to understanding where we've been and where we are going.

Evaluation therefore becomes a mix of both emotional and experiential reference points. What is character building for one individual becomes destructive for another. What one remembers as exciting and stimulating becomes unsettling and disturbing to another. Yet there is a lot of common ground too. The voices say again and again they would like their children to have the same kinds of opportunities they had as children. Not just for the travel, but for the depth of understanding they gained about the world in general and for the empathy they developed out there in it.

The legacy then is undeniably real. The adults growing out of these children have values, benchmarks and goals which are an inevitable result of their cultural mobility as children.

THE VOICES

Strengths That Came from the Family

Christine

As a child, I remember feeling free and independent. My friends and I would go into the villages to shop. We weren't ever really fearful of anything. We did what we wanted to do. In Islamabad we went into Rawalpindi. My parents weren't very strict. I'm sure they had their concerns, but I was never ... I didn't realize it at the time. I could certainly do what I wanted, or what I thought I wanted. I'm sure they had some kind of control, but it was never "No, you can't go here." We just had a good time. I had a horse and I was busy riding every day. That was in Pakistan and Laos. So I always had something to keep me busy.... In Pakistan we did lots of swimming.... It was just loads of fun, I thought. I had a great time as a kid.

Peter

I think the only time I had to fight for my own integrity was during that ninth grade year when I lived with my grandfather. Other than that ... I think to a very large extent it is because of my parents, my father's really strong sense of treating me not as a child, but very much as an equal, but not totally as an equal. He was definitely my father and the authority in my life. I had no idea of how I got this idea, but I said "I want to be a missionary in Korea." I was six years old. They came to me one day and said, "Do you remember, you said you wanted to be a missionary in Korea?" "Well, you're going to be one." My first question was, "What about you guys? Will you be able to come too?" They would often tell that story.

The idea was that for me, they always treated my desires as very real things. I never felt like they were pushing me, or pulling me, around. What we did, we did as a family. That was something that was very important to my father. It's something he's encouraged me to do ... with my own family. The goal is to operate as a family, and we operate as a family seeking to do what God is calling us to do, calling us as a family to do. In no sense does he call one of us and not the others. So my father's call was really our family's call. And I was as much a part of that as he was and my mother was. So I've always had that as a really strong underpinning throughout my life. I was respected, he dealt with me with integrity.

Barbara

... I guess the best thing my parents gave me -- and I don't know how they gave it to me -- but I never felt I had to jump off the cliff just because everyone else was jumping off the cliff. I could sit back and say, "That's not for me." I never gave anyone a hard time about it. I got more flack about it than they did. It hurt and it was rough, but it was very character building. My father always said, "Stand by your principles." Now I wish we had more people that did. That really helps a lot, especially if you're traveling and moving. I think you have to be adaptable and tolerant, but I think you also have to know what your principles are. "Are you going to do this, are you going to do that?" I could have been a nightmare to my parents; my brothers, especially my middle brother, really thought I would be. He kept saying "You can't move her around this much. You can't do this to her. She's going to have incredible psychological problems." It just didn't happen. Maybe I was just born that way.

How It Was for Us; How We'd Do It
for Our Own Children

<u>Christine</u>

I would definitely want my children to experience the world. I will never, ever have them stay in one place. I want them to get experiences, I want them to know different cultures. I would never want to limit them to one area, that's too closed off.

I treasure my childhood experiences now. It was both a good and bad experience. You learn things and you have knowledge that other people can never ever possibly have. On the other hand, you don't have a sense of security, you don't have the feeling of growing up with the same friends all your life, of bonding. That was always really, really hard for me. I never, ever felt a part of anything. Even now, but now I'm more tolerant, more accepting. If I tell people, and they get that sort of glazed look about them, I just go on. I don't expect them to understand.

But do other people like me have problems with memory of certain places? I think I have gaps where I just can't recall anything. I have to really rely on my mother to tell me. "What was it like there? What did I do?" I think once I left one country, I would block it out and focus on the next one. I think I was so disoriented, I just wanted to get a sense of a place and just belong. I wanted to forget about the other places I had been. Now I ... now I feel like I really should have paid attention more when I was growing up to the surroundings, the languages. I could have five different languages under my belt now. It's always been, "Well, if you don't want to learn, that's fine." "Tell me to do it!" That's what I missed the most.

Craig

I'm pretty much main stream at this point. I'm much more integrated into American society than I was during my 30s and 20s when I was jumping around so much. I think that as you get older, and especially when you reach 40, you kind of assess where you're at and realize that what you have is what you are going to get. Your options are more limited than when you are in your 30s. You can't just go on going from job to job. Everybody eventually reaches a point where they say "Well, this is the hand that's been dealt me." Enough is enough. Also, a lot of time has transpired since my childhood overseas. All of those things combined have caused me to be just a little more laid back. I think I know myself a lot better now than I did. I'm much more sure of myself. I've had some success. These past five years I've been very successful. That period in the camera industry -- 11 years -- was just a horrible period because I never felt successful. I never felt it was an occupation I was suited for. So there was always that internal tension. Now I feel I have a job I do well.

I would tell parents who are raising children overseas today to be much more attuned to the feelings of their children, at least more than my parents ever were. Even though the kids may not be verbalizing their feelings, believe me, they are probably going through a lot more turmoil than parents know about. Parents for the most part have had a stable upbringing, they have their stability, they have their roots. Mobile parents are not providing that to their children -- there is a big gap, a big difference in their upbringing and that of their children. I think they really need to be sensitive to that. Selling off the children's belongings in preparation for a move may not seem much to them, they see it only as material goods, but there are connections there -- there are feelings and sensitivities there that they really need to respond to. These feelings stay with the children for many, many years. They don't go away. In my case it had an effect

on me. It affects how the kids adjust much later -- maybe years later.
Kids' feelings don't necessarily end with a three year tour. What
happens to a child when he is eight or nine tends to stay with him, at
least in the subconscious, for many years to come. This leaving of
friends is just traumatic, especially for teenagers -- leaving
relationships, boyfriends, girlfriends. It's very, very hard.

Andrea

        The advice I wish I could give to parents is to just respect your
kids' feelings. To realize ... I know my parents had some feelings of
sadness when they left places, but for a kid, it's a lot harder. The kid's
life centers on what is immediately around them, their friends. Let the
kids be sad about leaving, don't say that that's a bad thing. There is
such an ethic to keep going, the next place is going to be great. I
think that instead it's good to let them reminisce. If the kids really
show an interest in keeping in touch with their friends, maybe their
parents could help them keep connected for a while. I think it is hard
for children to keep it up. We've done that with my son already when
he's made transitions from day care situations to being in nursery
school. It's hard to go where you always have to redefine everything.
        I wouldn't want my kids to have the same experience I had.
On the other hand, I can't say it's been all bad. I enjoy traveling and
I feel comfortable traveling. I like going places.

Peter

        I think about how different my life was from my children's; I
think about the things they're missing, things that I'd like them to
experience. But I'm also grateful for the things they are experiencing
(like) living here in this house, going to this school. They don't have
a sense of the seriousness of life that I grew up with. Sometimes I feel
like I would like to instill that in them.   But I'm not sure how to do

that. I don't want to be overbearing. These are some of the things I think about. We spend time together and we make a point of trying to teach them, to play together as a family.

Sally

I would tell families raising kids overseas today to make sure their children are in a good school.... I feel it is important that the kids have the experiences, but I know from my own experience that most kids will probably rebel at any kind of change. I know that in some cases living overseas has been a very good experience and in some other cases a really bad experience. Some kids need that stability of living in one place their whole life and some kids can handle the change better than others. I don't know how you know that until it actually happens. So I don't know what kind of advice I would give; you just have to hope they will adjust and try to make the most of this new city, or new town, or new country that they are living in. Try to show them that this new place can have a lot to offer, and can be very exciting, and they could learn a new language. Those were things my parents told me when we moved to Mexico, "You have this great opportunity to learn Spanish." But I never did. Parents can tell you things and can see things that their children can gain from, an experience that kids can't see when it's right on top of them. A close family helps. I think a lot of times kids will just have to adjust on their own. Parents are going to have to understand that it may not be an easy adjustment, but to just hang in there. I had one friend who used to live in Mexico and he and his brother, once they moved there, complained and hated it and didn't want to be there. They were miserable. So the father put in for a transfer and by the time the transfer came around the kids absolutely loved it and didn't want to leave. So I just think it's important that the parents stick with their goals for their family. Unless it's something just absolutely terrible that's happening to their kids, just stick with it.

I have to say that I seem to be more tolerant than most people I know. I have a broader understanding because I know how other people live, and I know what it is like to be picked on because I am different. That's not a nice feeling to be judged based on prejudice rather than fact. Just the general experience was valuable.

Sarah

In terms of how my past has influenced who I am, I have, or so it seems, always sided with the underdog and given the benefit of the doubt. Is this because I know all too well what it is like to be the "stranger in a strange land?" I don't know.

Barbara

I want my children to love to travel, although by the time I die I don't think there will be any exotic places left in the world. I want them to love to be adaptable, and I want them to learn a second language at a young age. I want them to be tolerant. I want them to be able to go into any situation and be tolerant and accepting of the people that they're with. I think I am very tolerant of people, but that doesn't mean that I would want to be like them, or necessarily approve of what they do, but I'm tolerant and would never condemn them.

I think learning adaptation skills is the best thing that could have happened to me. We lived in all former British colonies, with the exception of Switzerland and Norway, where people spoke English better than Americans anyway. I didn't learn foreign languages -- French and that was it. I can't say that language was the best thing I learned. Adaptability and tolerance were the best things I learned and also the sense that everything you do is an adventure, it's not a hardship, it's interesting. I learned that from my parents and from moving. That has helped me in so many situations.

Michael

... I always feel a little torn about that since I feel there were a lot of positive things I got out of growing up overseas and all the exposure I got to foreign countries. I think, "Gee, I want my kids to have that." I don't know how I'll reconcile that one, but ... that's the reason I've never been able to put out of my mind that I'll never go overseas again.

Gail

I think now I am almost open minded to a fault. I had the worst time because I could just see everybody's side of the argument, and I can still do that. Except at this point I am now able to form my own opinions out of seeing all those sides. It's really been a help to me in my work because I can absolutely put myself in that person's place and understand where they're coming from in their culture, and be able to see their point of view and why they insist on holding this position. Unfortunately in the past, it used to work against me because I could never discriminate among those positions and make a choice myself. That lasted until about age 25. What it meant was that I kept my mouth shut and never had an opinion. I think that's why my face doesn't have a lot of lines in it ... because I never had a lot of opinions until I was 25. Lines are marks of personality and expression, and I never had any. I really think that was an advantage in many ways, but it caused a lot of personal difficulties for me, because it was so agonizing to see everybody's point of view and not have a position yourself. Part of it was my personality, part of it must have been the lifestyle. You've been exposed to the fact that there is more than one way to think about something, and sometimes you've learned that maybe that other way is better. You'll come to question in the future whether you'll always strongly hold to this, because in the past it's been proven that just because you hold to it strongly doesn't mean it's the most useful position for you to take.

My ability to adapt has probably come in handy in school admissions. First of all, my training as the daughter of a diplomat has really come in handy. Even my friends in Peace Corps notice that when we had to negotiate our way through a border or something like that, they would usually leave it to me because I'm so good at making sure nobody got insulted, everybody still had their "face" when we left, and the guy who was being a jerk was able to be turned around because I was so respectful. "You're the one that has all the information. What do you think we could do to solve this problem? I wonder if you could help us." All of that stuff came right out of my training as being a little ambassador for my country. In that sense I acquired a lot of skills that I've since used professionally to great advantage.

Julia

I can hardly talk about what is happening in Yugoslavia at the moment. I was a child there. Part of the problem of growing up this way is that it is very hard to go back and test your childhood impressions against the realities of the day. You lose your childhood when you grow up. Normally you could go back and check for yourself. Now I am watching this place where I grew up destroyed and I literally can't stand to watch it. It's not as if I have any great attachment to the place now -- I only spent three and some years there, important years -- but I was a child there. I feel as though I have to work hard to keep all these various influences in my life integrated, and to adjust, but not to completely lose the childhood experiences either. To see the place physically destroyed seems symbolic.

<u>Peter</u>

Ever since we first started out in Korea, it has been one vast, wonderful experience. I've enjoyed the various situations. Part of the enjoyment -- at least when I got to be a teenager -- was in knowing that I could eventually tell these stories to somebody.

CHAPTER TEN

A FEW AMAZING STORIES, WELL TOLD

Introduction

Family stories, personal stories, are the threads that make up the fabric of life history. The voices had some good ones to share. They illuminate, perhaps better than any other one thing, the special vagaries of their childhood experiences. Some are about violence and war, some are about special privileges, some are about just being close to history in the making.

Our personal family favorite was an event which took place in Norway. My young daughters and I were walking in a woods near Oslo one cool, autumn afternoon and we ran into two gentlemen with a dog. Since my dog was also along, I took precautions to heel him in on his leash. But the dogs met and did their little male dog-dance while we greeted the men. Instinctively I used English for some reason rather than Norwegian. The older of the two men responded in excellent English and seemed pleased to comment on the weather and the beauty of the woods around us. Only after they walked on and my younger daughter asked "Who was that, Mommy?" could I explain to them that was King Olaf of Norway. I had made a major social and cultural blunder by talking with him at all, but he had understood right away we were American, not Norwegian, and therefore outside his realm. His English was natural; his mother, Maude, was one of Queen Victoria's daughters.

THE VOICES

Perks and Pranks

<u>Rob</u>

Mrs. Thoroughgood, ... the flat landlord in London, said, "Why Robbie, come here I've got something to tell you. The Beatles -- they're upstairs." Apparently the Beatles had moved in upstairs into the top flat. They were filming, or getting ready to film, "A Hard Day's Night." I thought she was joking. My sister was an autograph hound at the time, and she said, "Go up and get their autographs." So I got into the lift, went up to the top floor and knocked on the door. Sure enough, the door opened -- on a security chain -- and there were the four Beatles and Brian Epstein standing right there. I said, "Can I have your autograph?" I think they were just shocked, at first. They shut the door, took the chain off, and said "Where'd you come from?" I said I lived on the second floor. "Can I have your autograph?" I was sort of nonchalant. I suppose I could have ingratiated myself, but I was just in awe. I said "Thank you very much" and got back into the lift. Right behind me were Ringo, McCartney and George Harrison in the lift. I guess they just couldn't believe what happened, so they came down to see. "You're a Yank," they said. "Yeah," I said. I remember him asking me what they should wear to Washington. I said, "Well, it's cold. Bring a fur." I got off the lift and said "Cheerio."

I'll never forget coming back to the States -- I brought the autographs with me and some records -- and of course the Beatles hadn't been to the States yet. I remember going to a party over the holiday and taking some of their records over, an EP, which is an extended play with two 45s on either side. I remember taking it to a party and all the kids I was with -- I was 12 years old I guess --saying

"'Twist and Shout' and 'I Want to Hold Your Hand,' that's for kids." Well, the following week the Beatles appeared on tape on the Ed Sullivan show and it was said that they would appear live next week. And sure enough, two weeks later they appeared live and "I Want to Hold Your Hand" and "Twist and Shout" went to number one. I went back to England and the Beatles came back to England and lived there on the top floor -- everyone except for John Lennon since he was married to Cynthia Lennon at the time. They would leave every morning ... to go do their filming around London. They would come and go and people would leave their autograph albums or something for them to autograph out on the table downstairs. It got to the point where ... the first two months it was fun, I'd say hello. But the secretaries that worked in our offices right across the street, which again was a converted row house, saw them coming and going. After a while they had to have rent-a-cops and valet guards to keep peace. I'll never forget being stampeded by a group of girls because I'd come home in my loden coat with the hood down and I was playing this up -- all the screams! I came back one other time with groceries and was stampeded at the door. The door flew open, there were girls running up and down the halls, and that's when they finally got help.... We went to see "A Hard Day's Night" when it debuted at the Odeon on Piccadilly Square.

There were a lot of things taking place. The British were creating the best entertainment, the best rock groups. I remember going to a place called Tiles up in Soho, and a place called the Marquis Club and watching Jimmy Hendrix. I was running around with Andy Morrison, Jim Morrison's brother. Andy's father was an admiral in the Navy at the time. Andy kept running away from home trying to hook up with Jim -- Jim Morrison of the Doors. The Doors were a counter-culture rock group here in the States.

I still miss the liberalness of England, doing things we'd be jailed for here. They weren't crimes, they were larks. The English have a wonderful way of doing things that are considered larks. There is something called "rag week" where the college students run around and collect money to give to their favorite charity. They'll pull stunts, like kidnap so-and-so from a dinner and take him hostage for ransom, or they'll stop traffic for publicity. If you did any of those things here you'd get arrested.

For example, when I was about 15 my friend Chris and I -- this is when the spooks and spies were about -- followed this one gentleman for a while ... (and) we followed him for three or four hours. He called the police. He was just an ordinary pedestrian. He got quite concerned. We were playing games. When we came out of the pub after following him in, he said, "The bobbies are after you." Uh-oh. We split, going two different directions around the block. I turned the corner and here's Chris walking toward me and there is a cop right behind him, and, I don't see that there's a cop behind me. So they said, "You Yanks, what are you up to?" I said, "We're just having a lark." "Well, you owe someone an apology," one said. So we went back and apologized. We were just playing at James Bond. It was a little craziness.

Craig

We were talking earlier about how difficult it is for kids who have never grown up overseas to identify with what we went through. When I was in Bolivia I was dying to learn how to drive. I was 14. Some of my friends were a little older and starting to fool around with cars. So I begged my father to get me a Bolivian learner's permit. You could pretty much do whatever you liked there. He sent his Bolivian assistant over to get my learner's permit; he comes back with a permit that says I have passed my test, I'm allowed to drive. It has a picture on it and it's stamped by the Police Department. The only stipulation on it was that it had to be reviewed once a month. Somebody was getting some kickback out of this. I showed it to a friend of mine and he said "Hey, this is great. I want to get one too, but I don't want to have to renew mine, that's a hassle." So he sends out his butler with two bottles of Johnny Walker to the Police Station. He gets back a permanent license -- at 14. One time when my parents were out of town I actually did take the car. It was a stick shift. I only knew how to drive in one gear. So I am driving up a hill and these two Bolivian policemen stop me. I'm going the wrong way, in first gear, because I didn't know how to shift. I'm wondering what my parents would do. In the end, it cost three dollars and thank you very much. This is just an idea of what goes on over there.

On the Road

Peter

The second year we were at the Abbey a young Korean boy, about my age, was there for a few weeks. We had to get some supplies and he went with me into town. We got a lift in and then didn't have any transportation back. We had to walk back and I was carrying a sack of flour on my shoulder, the two of us walking down the highway -- this American and this Korean kid in the wilds of the country. Not far away some caverns had been discovered that just at that point had become news. They were the largest caverns in the Orient, or something like that. It was a place I had actually been to a couple of times. But at this point it got a lot of publicity. A minibus, which had been chartered by a group of Western reporters, passed us on its way to the caverns. The reporters looked out of their windows and saw this American kid walking down the road with a sack of flour on his shoulder. They started asking questions. "Oh yeah -- they live in this little valley up there, nobody quite knows what they are doing or why they are there or anything." A few days later a couple of reporters came by the Abbey and they wrote an article about pioneering (and) about the community. These were just ideas that grabbed peoples' imaginations. So we got this publicity and people started streaming up there. Over the years, it's been a nonstop flow. They come from all over the world, from all over Korea; many different churches send people up there for training or conferences. Currently they have about 6,000 visitors a year. Many people come and spend longer periods of time, some for ten or fifteen years now. Others come for a few days.

Of Mobs and Civil Chaos

<u>Julia</u>

One major influence in my life was that you couldn't grow up in Yugoslavia without being touched by the fact that so many people were hurt during the war. You would see people with terrible scars, a patch on their eye, limbs missing. Big buildings were still rubble, there were signs of the civil war, there was evidence of destruction everywhere, and it shocked me, coming from Arlington, Virginia. I became very interested in what caused all this. I am also half-Jewish and there was a small Jewish community, a very international community -- French, American, Italians. They celebrated their very existence. We celebrated Passover with them, which is a celebration of freedom, and it was very impressive to me as a child, the meaning these people gave to it. As a result, the meaning of the war was so real for me, the horror and the reality of the holocaust. I still feel one generation removed from my generation in America because my contemporaries have no sense of this. They grew up with their parents' war stories, but for me it was much more real and much more horrible. I just have a much more personal connection.

Andrea

Russia was a really hard place for me to be. My dad said, and we heard from school too, that there were microphones in the walls. There was a type of paranoia. I remember going to my dad's office and seeing all these papers in his in and out boxes, and I thought that if I actually read one of these papers out loud that would be like giving away secrets....

In the beginning I don't think I really knew what to be afraid of. I remember having nightmares and the thing that was hard about it was that I was having nightmares and getting scared and I really didn't have anyone to talk to about it.... My mom was really trying very hard to learn Russian.... She went to a lot of things with my dad, they were gone a lot at night. She was pretty much unavailable in a lot of ways. I just felt isolated, I guess.

We actually ended up being at the embassy when a demonstration was going on and that was really scary.... We happened to be there for the demonstration because the commissary was there. Normally we wouldn't be at the embassy. But we had gone there to go shopping. It was a big African demonstration -- African people against the United States. You know the Russians used to orchestrate a lot of demonstrations. There were a lot of Africans and they would get people all riled up and kind of manipulate them to do what they wanted them to do. We parked at the embassy and I remember walking across the courtyard -- maybe it was after we'd been to the commissary because they wouldn't have let us in if they'd known what was going on. We walked across this square courtyard and there was this big gate, tall bars on it. There were people climbing the gate and yelling and shouting all these things. It was so frightening. There were two MPs standing there passively with their guns, not pointing at anybody, but just standing there. And these people are climbing the gate and looking so angry and so violent. It was really scary. I think seeing any people climbing the gate was really frightening, like they were scaling a wall and getting ready to come in. That's what it felt like. And you only have these two people to defend you. And I'm sure that they did look strange to me being African.

We ended up staying with some friends inside their apartment inside the compound. We couldn't go home while this was happening. The demonstrators were throwing ink bottles at the windows and breaking the windows, leaving terrible stains and stuff. We were peeking out of the blinds. They were shouting things. It was very scary.

Then to know that my father would be out in this crowd. Not in that crowd -- he would have stood out! I can't remember what language they were yelling in. I don't know, it may have been a foreign language. That was very frightening for me. I don't know really why, but I never really talked about how it felt to me going through this to my parents, at least not until much later. I never got the reality balance. When I did tell my dad about it much later, he said that those things were so controlled that the next day the exact number of panes of glass that had been broken would be delivered to the embassy. I don't think they told them to break 20 windows, but they were obviously watching the whole thing and at no point was there really any danger that something would happen. But as a child, watching it, it didn't feel like that.

I remember the whole time there (in Russia) just being scared. Cars would go by, there would be shadows in your room -- you know, when you're a little kid, there's always shadows in your room and things move. I would try and go to sleep and just think about going on a bus, just the regular routine and then it would change and people would be coming out of the walls and things like that ... grabbing, grabbing. It was mostly our family. We'd be sitting around a table and people would be grabbing us, then I would wake up.

Rob

    We were evacuated from Tel Aviv for the Suez Canal crisis in 1956 or `57. We were given six hours to pack. We threw everything into steamer trunks -- one trunk per person. I remember being told to get some rest, but the lights were on, everyone was running around the house packing, tanks were rolling up and down the street, my mother was crying because she didn't know what was going on and what was going to happen.

    ... I'll still never forget forming a convoy. We had to meet at four in the morning on the beaches in Israel. All the dependents of the French, Italian and American embassies met and we rode up to Haifa where the CIA had apparently commandeered an Italian ocean liner to get us out of there quickly. I think the Arabs knew what was going on -- that civilians were being evacuated --because they allowed us the opportunity to leave. Everyone was on the boat, you could see the men on the pier, and it was very sad to see all these women and children on the boat waving. Not ten minutes after we left the port, it was bombed. Apparently a submarine was involved. When they lowered the net to allow the ship out of the port of Haifa, the sub went in and there was an explosion. There was a lot of concern on the ship about the men, but they radioed back to say that everything was fine. It was a terrorist attempt, but all the fathers were OK. The mood in the dining room that evening was very somber and quiet, you could hear a pin drop There were only women and children in this ornate ocean liner dining room. It was just a very unusual experience. I got sea sick for the first time. The Mediterranean is described as a bathtub, and that's just what it was. It's a very rough ocean. In fact the captain even came down the cabins to reassure everyone that this was OK. He asked me if there was anything he could do for me, and I asked if he would stop the boat and let me get off!

In Cyprus first we stayed in an old World War II barracks.... They were wooden and they hadn't been lived in since the war. It was very temporary. There were some that chose to stay there, closer to Israel; Cyprus is not that far. Those that protested were sent to Rome at State Department request. We got on another boat and went to Rome via Athens.... I remember that the State Department found a hotel for the dependents, but children weren't allowed in this hotel. So the children had to use the back entrance. Children should be not seen and not heard. I remember having to go around this hotel to the back entrance and slowly going up to the hotel room.

Andy

The summer after my freshman year at Carleton I went back to visit my parents in India.... From there I went on to Lebanon in September. I had traveled around India with my girlfriend that summer as well. I got a chance to visit the village where she was born and raised. We said goodbye and I went on to Lebanon. She was supposed to go back to college herself in Colorado. But she decided to pay me a surprise visit in Lebanon on her way back.

I was there on top of the mountains in (the) little village of Shemlan where they have the American language program. It overlooks the airport, the international airport of Beirut. I was about 3,000 feet up and the airport is at sea level. One day I heard on the radio there was a hijacking. I looked down and there on the tarmac was a British Airways plane. This was the first big hijacking by the Palestinians over the liberation of Palestine. They had taken four planes at once, so for a time I saw this British Airways plane on the tarmac and then it took off and flew to an abandoned British military airfield in the middle of the desert in Jordan. One of the other planes was blown up in Cairo, but the other two were flown to Jordan too. For four days these hostages were held inside the planes in the heat of the desert. We were listening to the news all this time.

On the fourth day, I was informed by the embassy that my girlfriend was on that plane! They put that together because her parents knew that she had taken that flight. They got in touch with my parents, and my parents then informed the embassy in Beirut. I think I was informed literally as I knew that they had just released the women and children on the planes. The next day they released the men and then blew up the planes. She was first taken to Amman and then to Cyprus and then to the States. I didn't see her until the next summer. The bizarre thing was that the Popular Front for the Liberation of Palestine (PFLP) was Marxist oriented and headed by George Habash, a Palestinian. They represented the university educated, intellectual Palestinians. I was very sympathetic to the Palestinian cause. As a child I had heard my parents talk about it, in high school I'd persuaded them to let me take off classes and write an independent study on the Palestinian problem my last semester. In Beirut I had a Palestinian roommate who had grown up in a refugee camp.

That week, after all this was over, I was in Uncle Sam's restaurant, a little hang-out near the university -- a famous little restaurant that served hamburgers -- and I was introduced to a guy in the next booth who was a huge, rotund, Palestinian who spoke with an Oxford accent because he was educated at Oxford. He was a member of the PFLP, and had been directing some of the operations that day from the airport tower. He was introduced to me as "the man who...". So I sat down with him and we had this bizarre conversation in which I said ... "my girlfriend!..." I asked if he would have harmed her and he said, "Well, no, it was all to get publicity, we never would have killed them. At the worst we may have taken them off the plane and walked them into the hills and held them hostage for a little longer. But we have no other way to get the world's attention."

Barbara

When the war started in Cyprus my parents were out of the country and I was staying with a Turkish family.... While my parents were outside the country they didn't know I had gone to the Turkish sector, they didn't know where I was. They thought I would still be with the Turkish family in our house. But they were worried. The family were Turkish Cypriots and they were very good friends of ours. They agreed to take care of me and take care of the house while my parents were gone for two weeks. I loved Cyprus so much that whenever they left, I didn't want to go. They went back for my brother's wedding, and I stayed on Cyprus.

It was really bad for the Turkish family staying with us because all our neighbors were either Greek or Armenian, and these residents were telling the soldiers that there were Turkish spies living in our house. That's why they took me back to their house in the Turkish zone. They were in fear of their lives. When we got to the Turkish sector they started saying that they didn't think my parents would be able to get back into the country because the situation was worsening. They said maybe I should start leaning Turkish, and they would adopt me. I was being taught Turkish and I was being brought into their family life. They were under a great deal of stress. Members of their family were in the army, they didn't know what to do about me, they didn't have any money; nobody had money suddenly. The war had just started and then it escalated. It was really a horrible thing. I don't think Americans know what it's like. I don't know -- even though I was in that situation and saw them go through that stress -- I don't really know what it would be like if our country was at war. They were concerned that they should take care of me for my parents and they felt betrayed when the UN came and insisted that they take me back over to the Greek side. That was really hard. They also started treating me not as nicely as they used to, I think because of the stress they were under.

I did worry that my parents wouldn't be able to find me. All I suddenly knew was what these people were telling me, and I saw a different side to them and it frightened me. As it happened, one of their sons was killed soon after I left them. So the stress was very real. There were food shortages too and they were poor.

My parents couldn't get back into the country. My father was working for the United Nations Development Program, so the UN had a convoy sent into the Turkish sector to find me and take me out and take me to the Greek sector. It was two UN cars with flags and everything, and we had to go back through these checkpoints.... I stayed with a French family until my parents were able to catch the last flight in, on an Israeli airline into Cyprus. After a day, they were able to locate me. Then we moved back into our house and the Turks invaded the next morning. I woke up to a bullet ricocheting across my bed. I still have the bullet somewhere. We picked it out of the wall afterwards -- I keep it as a good luck charm. We were barricaded in our house. My father got all the mattresses from upstairs and he barricaded his study and we slept on a mattress for two nights and listened to the BBC and VOA to learn when there would be a ceasefire so we could go where we needed to go.

One morning I remember waking up -- they were bombing and shooting all night long when the Turks invaded -- and nobody was in the study. The radio was still on, softly. The fear of God went through me, I thought maybe my parents had been taken away. I couldn't figure out what had happened. There were still bullets going off, and there was glass on either side of the entry door and I had to cross that entry hall to get into the rest of the house. I finally just ran for it, hoping no bullets would be shot through at that time. Fortunately my parents were in the living room, just sitting on the floor. They got out of the study because they were just getting so claustrophobic. I can remember thinking, "Oh, God, where are they?" I was so petrified. We had an anti-aircraft gun on the corner of our street, we were one house away from that corner. The house on that corner was bombed, and the house diagonally across from us was bombed....

A ceasefire was announced and we drove to the Hilton Hotel and joined a convoy to Dhekelia, a British Camp.... There were dead bodies and blown artillery along the route.... We stayed at the British camp for two or three weeks, sleeping on cots.

We finally got to Zurich -- we knew Zurich, it was so nice to get there, life was so nice there. We checked into a hotel on the park and had a nice bath and a three course expensive meal, my father ordered lots of wine and champagne. It was delightful.

APPENDIX

A Note On Methodology

To structure the interviews with the various voices heard in this book I developed a list of talking points which helped focus the dialogue. Not all questions were relevant to each person interviewed.

Before the interviews I gave a copy of the talking points to the interviewee and asked them to mark for me which questions they would particularly like to talk about, which questions grabbed at their innards.

Talking Points

1) Tell me what you can remember about your childhood, hitting the high points and the low points as best you can.

Identity
- A)   Have you felt yourself to be a minority?
- B)   Did you ever think of yourself as "different?"
- C)   Were you born overseas or in America?
- D)   If born overseas, how do you feel about that?
- E)   Do you have a desire now to return to the countries where you lived as a child? Why?
- F)   Do you identify easily with other Americans?
- G)   How strong were your childhood ties to places and family in America or elsewhere?
- H)   How did you answer the question: "Where are you from?"
- I)   Can you describe your father's or mother's work overseas?
- J)   Was your identity linked to your parents' status? How?
- K)   Who were your childhood friends -- their nationalities, their interests, their language of choice?

L)   You are a baby boomer -- how do you see yourself in relation to this group?

M)   Is your religion part of your identity? How?

Language

A)   Do you think in English or in another language?

B)   How does that affect your reasoning in English?

C)   What is your mother's first language?

D)   Do you find it easy to learn languages?

E)   Did you use a language other than English with your childhood friends?

F)   How are you using your language skills now?

Transitions

A)   How did you usually find out the family was preparing to move?

B)   Were you powerless over the decision or have input into the decision?

C)   How did you express grief for the people and places you were leaving behind?

D)   How did you feel if you had to leave pets behind?

E)   How did it feel to leave a local caretaker?

F)   Can you ever remember having an expectation of a new place realized or unrealized.

G)   Did an impending move excite or depress you?

H)   Did you ever experience a sense of relief to leave a certain place? Why?

Education

A)   Describe your formal education?

B)   Did it meet your expectations?

C)   How have you used it as an adult?

D)   What kinds of skills do you think you gained growing up as you did?

Family matters
  A)   Do you have siblings, if so, how many? Are you
        first, middle, last?
  B)   How would you describe your relationship with your
        siblings?
  C)   Describe your relationship with your parents.
  D)   Can you describe your parents' relationship?
  E)   Do you know why your family chose to live overseas?
  F)   How did your parents like living overseas?

2)   Can you describe how it feels to go through re-entry into
      America?
  A)   How did re-entry affect you?
  B)   Did you feel a loss of "status" on return? Explain.
  C)   How did re-entry affect your self-image and
        identity?
  D)   How did it feel to no longer be a "guest in the
        country?"
  E)   How did it feel when the funding organization paid
        your last ticket home?

3)   Describe how you feel now about the experiences you
      had as a child.

4)   How have those experiences impacted on your choices
      as an adult? Can you see any relationship?

Career
  A)   How do you rate the importance of your career to
        your life?
  B)   Do you like what you are doing?
  C)   How long do you expect to do it?
  D)   What would you choose to do if you could choose to
        do anything?

E)   Does what you're doing now relate in any way to your
        childhood experiences? Explain.

Mobility/Stability
A)   Are you restless or content to stay put?
B)   How long have you lived where you live now?
C)   How long do you intend to stay there?
D)   Describe your community involvement.
E)   Would you say it's been easy or hard to put down
        roots? Explain.
F)   Why do you want (or not want) to stay where you are?
G)   Are you comfortable with your American identity?
H)   How do you exercise your responsibilities as a
        citizen?
I)   How do you answer the question "Where are you
        from?" now?
J)   Do you have the ability to feel comfortable almost
        anywhere in the world?
K)   Do you have a current passport? Do you use it
        often?

Relationships
A)   Do you seem to make friends easily?
B)   Do you still keep in touch with any childhood
        friends?
C)   Who are your friends now?
D)   Do you seek out people who have a "world view?"
E)   Do you seek out people who can share their roots
        with you?
F)   Describe your spouse or companion.
G)   How would you describe your relationship with your
        spouse or companion?
H)   How would you describe your relationship with
        your children?

I)   Do you work to keep friendships up?

J)   Are keeping or losing relationships a problem
      or no problem?

5) As a young adult did you ever experience a period
    of particular disequilibrium? If so, at what
    age and under what circumstances?

6) Have you ever sought psychological therapy?

7) Would you describe yourself as a joiner or a loner? Explain.
    If a joiner, does joining in give you the satisfaction
    of belonging? What kinds of groups do you join up with?

8) Do you try to control what happens to you or are
    you more fatalistic about what happens to you?

9) What role does religion have in your life?

10) If you could advise families raising children overseas
    today, what would you tell them?

11) Which country do you remember best? Why?

12) Did you ever experience terrorism, riots, or conflict while
    living overseas? How did it affect you?

13)   Did you experience family or other traumas as a child not
      connected to living abroad? If so, describe.

14) How do you visualize your future? Is it in
    terms of change or long-term stability?

15) If you could change one thing about your life, what would it be?

16) Would you want your children to be brought up the same way you were?

17) If your house was burning, is there any one object you would feel compelled to save above all others. Why?